To those with the desire, passion, and *H.E.A.R.T.* to lead.

The

H.E.A.R.T.

of

LEADERSHIP

Understanding Key Characteristics
Which Strengthen Organizational Capacity

Dr. Carla D. Brown

WESTBOW
PRESS®
A DIVISION OF THOMAS NELSON
& ZONDERVAN

WestBow Press books may be ordered through booksellers or by contacting:

WestBow Press
A Division of Thomas Nelson & Zondervan
1663 Liberty Drive
Bloomington, IN 47403
www.westbowpress.com
1 (866) 928-1240

ISBN: 978-1-9736-9535-6 (sc)
ISBN: 978-1-9736-9536-3 (e)

Print information available on the last page.

WestBow Press rev. date: 11/06/2020

CONTENTS

PREFACE

What are the qualities that one looks for in a leader? How do leadership characteristics impact organizational effectiveness? While successful leaders are capable of motivating others toward common goals, extraordinary leaders can create social order, change organizational culture, and complete the mission of an organization. Several theories seek to explain various leadership styles and their impact on how organizations function. It is the leadership style of the leader that plays an integral role in being able to sustain as well as transform organizations. Research has proven that leaders can inspire followers to accomplish goals through characteristics that are indicative of not only who they are but by what they do

To effectively achieve the mission of an organization, leaders must consider their most important resources, the workers, and ensure that they share the same espoused values as the leader. This book examines leadership character traits that are identified as critical to business operations and further explain how leadership characteristics motivate employees' efforts toward organizational goals.

INTRODUCTION

Many homes have what some would describe as curb appeal. At first glance, when viewing a home from the street, the house appears to be well built and just what the buyer was looking for, as far as houses go. However, after careful examination and upon going inside of the home, the prospective buyer discovers not only are there issues with the plumbing, but also water has damaged the foundation of the home. While these concerns were not visible when viewing the home from the exterior, they present major problems. The foundation of the home must be solid for the house to be able to stand. This is analogous to attempting to bake a cake without eggs or barbecuing on the grill without the main ingredient, the sauce. While baking, grilling, building homes, and running a company are vastly different, they each require a certain skill set which, when combined with their respective components, breeds success. One such example is the Starbucks Corporation, known for its premier coffee. The company's special ingredient has allowed their stock to climb 5,000 percent. Starbucks' recipe for success is a concept which helps the company exceed good, extend beyond great; it is an extraordinary company. Leadership experts Schultz and Yang credit the Starbucks corporation's success to their business model, along with the company's long-standing values, which draw customers regardless of the distance, competition, or even cultural practices. Starbucks has mastered the "Three P's": product, people, and processes that allow businesses an opportunity to be successful. Each ingredient plays an integral part in creating an environment that provides an ultimate customer service experience. As are the workers, the coffee is part of a well-run process from the bean to the cup; manufactured and delivered to over 27,000 Starbucks retail stores across the globe. Though the Starbucks headquarters is in Seattle, Washington, the corporation has 142,000 employees worldwide, maintaining five distribution centers in the United States, two distribution centers in Europe, and two in Asia. On top of all that is the secret sauce, which is the corporation's customer-driven focus. Though the success of Starbucks is not a secret, it is their secret sauce that allows the retail giant to serve over 500 customers per day in over 70 countries. While this book is not a story about how to become as profitable as Starbucks, it does seek to highlight aspects of leadership that makes Starbucks the successful corporation that it is today.

There are similarities as well as differences between Starbucks and other companies. When viewing companies such as Chick-fil-A, for example, there are more similarities than there are differences. Starbucks and Chick-fil-A both serve specialty grade coffee; one as a coffee enterprise and the other as a supplement to their menu. Each organization has notably happy workers. Studies show that employees of Starbucks and Chick-fil-A are among the lowest-paying restaurants yet have the happiest workers. This can be attributed to the fact that both companies are customer-oriented and place great emphasis on satisfying customers, workers, and stakeholders. For this reason, workers feel valued and are appreciative of intrinsic rewards though they may not receive financial rewards. While some businesses focus on the bottom dollar, the bottom line for Starbucks and Chick-fil-A is ensuring that workers enjoy the environment and are given opportunities for advancement within the workplace. Leaders for both companies demonstrate open communication between management and employees that provides transparency while allowing workers to feel like valuable members of the team. From this perspective, both Starbucks and Chick-fil-A employs workers who not only show up to do the work but are also happy to be there. This level of engagement and, ultimately the organizational success, is the result of effective leadership. Companies today require leadership with the capacity to drive their mission while simultaneously engaging in efforts to further develop and grow the business. Therefore, business leaders must ensure a certain group of skill sets and values to sustain as well as expand. Despite an ever-changing economy, Starbucks has remained stable and continues to grow worldwide. The company has an unmatched talent for putting people before profit, which ultimately drives the success of the business. It is the leadership style of the leader that plays an integral role in being able to sustain as well as transform organizations. To understand how the leadership style of the leader impacts an organization, we must first begin by defining leadership.

UNDERSTANDING LEADERSHIP

"Great leaders don't set out to be a leader...They set out to make a difference. It's never about the role — always about the goal."
~Lisa Haisha

Why do we need theories to explain leadership? Several theories seek to explain various leadership styles and their impact on the effectiveness of organizations. Some theorists argue that while leadership is widely observed, it is universally misunderstood. This is due in part to the common misperceptions, or assumptions, about leadership.

Basic Assumptions

There are assumptions about human nature that ultimately influence leadership. The Realist-Relativist-Contingency school of thought explains that there is a worldview of leadership which is conflicted due to several assumptions.

O'Toole's Basic Assumptions of Leadership:

- People are by nature evil and self-interested, thus they must be controlled;
- Human groups are given to anarchy;
- Progress comes from discipline, order, and obeying tradition;
- Order arises from leadership;
- There can only be one leader of a group;

- The leader is the dominant member of the group;
- Leadership is an exercise of power;
- Any sign of weakness will undercut the leader's authority;
- Loyalty, effort, and change can be commanded successfully (Stark, 2005, p. 13-14).

Basic assumptions about leadership create a distorted view of what leadership is and why it is necessary. It further perpetuates an illusion for individuals seeking leadership positions and determining the leadership style that best fits their organization. As a leader, it is necessary to develop a style of leadership that will allow him or her to lead others toward accomplishing the mission of the organization. Self-awareness allows leaders to recognize their capabilities as well as seek opportunities for personal and professional growth. Conscious leaders recognize who they are or who they need to become to strengthen the capacity of their organization.

What is Leadership?

Many leadership theories explain the individual impact that leaders have on the effectiveness of its organizations. Leadership experts Bruce Winston and Kathleen Patterson define leadership as the honest guidance and training led by a visionary who is capable of persuading others and obtaining buy-in to the mission of an organization. In other words, a leader must be able to persuade, or influence, individuals toward a specific goal. To effectively meet the goals of an organization the leader must be able to coach the followers and manage the group's productivity. This last part is worth repeating. Though there is a clear distinction between leadership and management, the two words are often misunderstood and used interchangeably. From a sociological perspective, leaders are viewed by what they represent. In other words, leaders are observed, symbolically, as a social force that brings about change or social order. Extraordinary leaders can create social order, ultimately changing the culture of the organization to complete the mission of the organization. To effectively achieve the mission of an organization, a leader must first consider the organization's most important resources: its workers. Likewise, leaders should ensure that organizational members' behaviors are aligned with the espoused values of the organization (Schein, 2010). What are the main qualities of a leader? Leadership experts J. Scott Duvall and J. Daniel Hays (2012) identify four main qualities that leaders possess as the following: honesty, forward-looking, competency, and inspiration (p. 36).

Leadership as a Calling

We must first recognize that leadership is a calling. The call to leadership bears a responsibility that allows individuals to inspire and influence others. While leadership roles are prominent, highly regarded positions, leadership positions can attract persons seeking to have the title, but for all of the wrong reasons. Leadership, by all accounts, is not for everyone. Researchers agree that, in most cases, individuals do not choose their life's work but are undoubtedly led to them. One can infer that, if we are open, we will be drawn to do exactly what we have been uniquely and purposely designed to do. We may have preconceived notions of the direction we would like to go or have desired goals for which decisions are based upon. While we are allowed to make choices, other aspects are inherently factored into those decisions. For instance, individual gifts, talents, and aptitude are all factors that extend beyond our natural desires. Those who are called into leadership are given capabilities that must be sustained to fulfill their God-given purpose. "You did not choose me, but I chose you and appointed you so that you might go and bear fruit - fruit that will last - and that whatever you ask in my name the Father will give you" (John 15:16). When leaders are called into their role, they are reminded not only does God call them to a specific purpose, but also, He will equip them with the capability to complete the mission.

DISCUSSION QUESTIONS

1. How would you describe your leadership style?

2. What do you believe are the top qualities of a leader?

3. How would your direct reports describe you as a leader?

LEADERSHIP VERSUS MANAGEMENT

In many leadership circles, the terms leader and manager are clearly outlined. Both may be considered forward-thinking and goal-driven. Leaders and managers alike may be viewed as charismatic and even likable. However, researchers have identified several characteristics that provide a distinction between leaders and managers. It should be noted that disparities exist among the impact that leaders have on their organization and the effect on followers by those who manage. Scholars compare the various behaviors of managers, who are task-driven, versus leaders, who inspire workers toward organizational goals while promoting personal and professional development. When comparing the actions of leaders versus managers, it provides a contextual reference for further understanding (Northouse, 2013, p. 7).

MANAGERS	LEADERS
Tell you what to do	Show you the way
Focus on profit	Focus on people
Instill fear	Inspire trust
Set daily goals	Envision the future
Have an 'I' mindset	Have a 'We' approach
Hear what you say	Listen empathetically
Look for someone to blame	Accept responsibility
Do things right	Do the right thing

(Adapted from Northouse, 2013)

Effective leaders recognize the value of service to others. While the bottom line for some managers is making a profit, leaders such as the head of Starbucks believe in placing people over profit. When leaders value people over profit, success follows. Moreover, successful leaders recognize the need to invest in developing workers. This can be accomplished through various strategies to include leadership development programs as well as mentoring and coaching.

Mentoring and Coaching

Mentoring and coaching workers is a best practice that provides employees with a sense of inclusion, value, and growth. Mentor leadership fosters a mindset that is not only focused on the leader but the people whom they serve. This approach allows an employee to have one-on-one attention, guidance, and support in an effort to enhance individual capabilities, increasing organizational performance as a whole. When leaders invest in their workers, it benefits the individual as well as the organization. Coaching is a style of leadership that lends itself to viewing the performance of the team as a whole. Coaching leadership is a leadership style in which followers are developed and empowered to work as a team. Extensive research has been conducted to examine the effectiveness of coaching leadership. Findings yield that, while team-building exercises did not prove to enhance overall team performance, a team coaching approach proved to be more beneficial, as well as sustainable. Having an internal or external coach for team members allows for continuous performance improvement. Scholars point out that mentoring focuses on human development while coaching focuses on daily behavior towards improvement. Organizations benefit when leaders recognize the impact that mentoring and coaching has on the effectiveness of an organization. Scripture highlights the fact that "Iron sharpens iron, and one man sharpens another" (Proverbs 27:17). The significant impact of mentoring and coaching on organizations cannot be negated for we know that "Iron sharpens iron, and one man sharpens another" (Proverbs 27:17).

DISCUSSION QUESTIONS

1. What are the similarities and differences between coaching and mentoring?

2. Do you agree that there is added value in coaching and mentoring workers? If so, identify the benefits as it applies to your organization.

3. How do you plan to cultivate this practice within your organization?

OVERCOMING ROADBLOCKS

Today's leaders face many challenges. A concern for many leaders is keeping employees engaged and motivated to perform. This becomes a balancing act for leaders to lead a team of productive workers while delivering quality service or products to all customers. Leaders, regardless of the organization, share common interests of providing vision and guidance to followers to accomplish organizational goals. When examining various types of organizations such as businesses, educational institutions, and military branches, the leaders all share unique qualities that define who they are. Ultimately, those same qualities help to set the tone of the organization. While the leader's leadership style is a driving force in guiding the mission of an organization, the organizational design is also a critical component for operating effectively and overcoming obstacles.

Organizational Design

Successful leaders understand organizations need a roadmap to help guide the mission of their organizations. To do this, leaders develop a strategy for the organization, using the structure as a vehicle. From this perspective, organizational design and strategy are interconnected. Strategy, therefore, is the baseline for ensuring the organization is operating effectively and efficiently while creating a design that provides the structure to achieve the goals. When strategy and design are in congruence, organizations have a model that is a perfect fit. In this environment, employees are given the proper resources and tools to do their job. While this sets employees up to perform successfully, consideration should be given to rewarding employees or offering incentives for their work. While scholars argue that organizational designs and incentives are interdependent, incentive programs should be considered when determining the flow of operations. Though the effectiveness or ineffectiveness of a design may not be determined until later, it is not uncommon to discover the design as it unfolds while monitoring its progress. Depending on the success or failure of the design, leaders can redesign, implementing a new approach.

Employee Performance

Business leaders observe many contributing factors for poor company performance. Explanations vary from blaming human capital to scrutinizing international politics. In other cases, the breakdown is a result of broken processes. Anne Mulcahy, CEO of the Xerox corporation, was able to take accountability for her company's performance and revealed that her company faced problems due to an unattainable business model. Several companies including Enron, Kmart, and WorldCom made this same mistake, attempting to justify mediocrity, therefore, creating a culture of victimization. The challenge is correcting the victim mentality to, instead, develop a reputation of a thriving business. With this in mind, the ability to influence others to perform should be at the forefront. This requires leaders to have a sense of self-awareness. Effective leaders have a keen sense of their personal qualities and skills. While there are arguments on both sides regarding whether or not natural-born leaders exist, there is research supporting the position that leadership traits are developed through an integrated approach of mentoring and other learning methods. Leadership development is integral to leaders being able to influence others to perform. Effective leaders ensure that they continually develop as leaders while empowering workers to make efforts toward achieving his or her fullest potential.

Many organizations develop and implement a rewards program

as an incentive to drive employee performance. The program is intended to motivate workers toward incentives, which may help increase productivity. Incentives are described as mechanisms used to influence an employee, or groups of employees', behavior. However, deciding to use an employee rewards program can present a set of challenges. Though organizational leaders may want to be decisive in implementing an incentives program, they will need to determine whether the rewards should be results-driven or behavior-driven. While rewards, based on employee behavior, are primarily concerned with workers remaining compliant with company regulations, results-driven incentives focus on employee performance (Burton, Obel & Hakonsson, 2015). Some organizations reward employees based on individual performance. Conversely, leaders may decide to reward groups of employees by recognizing entire units or departments. Depending on the organizational structure of a company, incentives for groups of people may be the course of action for offering rewards. While group recognition creates a system of unity amongst teams, it also fosters a group thinks culture (Ackermann & Eden, 2011). The danger of this occurrence is that efforts made could become counterproductive. From this perspective, group think could stifle creativity with members of the group to avoid having their ideas disregarded. As a result, social relationships become a priority over personal viewpoints being shared when working in groups.

Expect Setbacks

While leaders anticipate celebrating successes, they should also expect setbacks. A leader envisions his dream, reflects on his capacity to fulfill the goals, and with determination and passion strives to achieve the desired goals. However, when taking steps toward fulfilling the mission of an organization, leaders should both prepare for and expect setbacks. While failed experiences present challenges, these setbacks also allow opportunities for learning and reinventing. A key strategy when working towards building success involves appropriately responding when things do not go quite as planned. Successful leaders are capable of learning from their mistakes then continuing to recreate, reinvent and further expand. For example, the Minnesota Mining and Manufacturing Company (3M), in its 117-year history, has continued to innovate, developing a variety of products to be used worldwide. Part of 3M's growth process entails developing and testing new ideas then redesigning the products to further develop its concept. The company demonstrates the ability to grow and expand through successes as well as failures.

Through experimenting and not being afraid of setbacks, the 3M company has continued to grow. One such experiment that Home Channel News reveals is the testing process required for 3M's LeadCheck Swabs. The swabs were created to reveal whether paint contained lead. If the swab turned red, this was an indicator of the presence of lead. Initial testing began with painted wood and metal and was later approved for use on drywall and plaster. The 3M LeadCheck Swabs were recognized for its practicality, low cost, and absence of toxic chemicals (Home Channel News, 2012, p. 47). The quest to ensure safe environments in commercial businesses for Renovation, Repair, and Painting (RRP) projects is also an internal practice for 3M. To address safety concerns at their manufacturing plants, 3M has implemented systems to control the safety risks. The Prevent Accident with Safety (PAWS) program was created in 1999 then further developed in 2001, specifically to ensure workplace safety through a peer-to-peer accountability program. This approach involves plant employees observing the safe or unsafe practices of their colleagues then following up by having a conversation with their co-workers regarding the observed behavior. As a result of these practices, the company has improved its safety performance, having less reported incidents of injury to its workers. Being continuously innovative and implementing safety measures to build the capacity for further development and expansion sets 3M apart from other companies (Harvey, 2014, p. 51).

The company, as we know it today, did not reach this level of achievement overnight. 3M first began with an invention of sandpaper and later produced adhesive cellophane tape and masking tape along with photocopiers. To further enhance material durability and visibility,

3M began designing products that add value to electronic displays as well as office products such as notepaper and adhesive tape. By the 1950s, 3M expanded its products to create materials that could be used in the health care industry. Those materials included supplies used for surgery, dental and orthodontic needs. Additional expansions included protective mechanisms such as tamperproof packaging material and document protection. To further expand, the company acquired a 40,000 square-foot building that quadrupled its existing design space, offering multi-levels to further enrich and develop more products.

While many companies share a common goal of helping to enrich the lives of others through products or services, not every organization has such longstanding history as 3M. For example, ITT Technical Institute was able to sustain its operations for almost 50 years. The for-profit company gradually expanded its services over the decades and was able to maintain an advantage over many of its competitors. In the last 20 years of business, the company eventually grew to operate 150 locations across 38 states. Though there was rapid growth over one decade, there was a steady decline over the next. Was the school's downfall the result of poor leadership? Were there lessons to be learned from past failures that were overlooked? In 2016, the company filed for bankruptcy, ultimately closing its doors. To its detriment, the company was unable to review, analyze, and learn from their failures. These failures, in hindsight, offered opportunities for developing strategies to restructure and transform the organization.

When leaders design a structure that allows individual departments to function independently while collectively working towards organizational goals, it sets the organization up for success. Though setbacks may be inevitable, a well-balanced organization allows for oversight as well as accountability. Several examples exist of well-organized and structured organizations. One such example is the Center for Child and Family Studies (CCFS) under the College of Social Work at the University of South Carolina. The CCFS provides consultation and support to human service and child-serving agencies within the community. The organization operates from a unique set of values while striving to be the premier workforce development resource for community partners. This organization is comprised of credentialed and experienced staff amongst departments which provide research and evaluation, instructional design and materials, training, and quality assurance. The CCFS leadership team is cognizant of the need to maintain a core set of values and capabilities to sustain as an organization as well as remain competitive. Like 3M, the organization continuously examines ways to become innovative while building the capacity of the team. Innovation expert Gary Oster points out that through innovation, organizations reveal the spirit of Christ (2011, p. 3). This is aligned with Scripture that reminds us "Let each of you look not only to his own interests but also to the interests of others" (Philippians 2:4). While much of the success of the CCFS can be attributed to its products, people, and processes, the leader must be able to cultivate the culture, establish system processes, and perform continual analysis of previous performances that allows the agency to thrive.

Organizations have the potential to benefit from trial and error. While organizations are not exempt from experiencing failures, how the leaders react to those failures play a critical role in an organization's success. The 3M company is a prime example of both innovation and learning. The convergence of the two has allowed the company to sustain itself for 117 years while continually developing products and expanding their brand. When leaders review and analyze their work and are capable of learning from failed products, they build the propensity for success. This key factor is the first step towards reshaping, restructuring, and recreating. Regardless of whether it's a new venture or new ideas for an existing company, the capacity for leadership to be agile and responsive to failure breeds success for organizations.

Resistance to Change

Workers foresee change as an intrusive infringement upon their social relationships within the organization. Amid organizational change, the culture within the organization may shift. Though leaders may observe certain reactions to organizational change before the changes occur, change leaders often do not anticipate dealing with behaviors after the change process is completed. It is common for organizational changes to evoke emotions that drive behaviors. This is explained as human behavior which, depending on circumstances, people act first, then attribute meaning to the shown behavior. This parallels with the notion that external factors impact a person's actions. Regardless of the reaction to change, organizational change continually occurs and gets even more complex depending on a company's size and structure. Change agents must be cognizant of behaviors that are not altered after the implementation of new goals and means as well as reward and control systems. The trick for organizational leaders is being able to move past the resistance to avoid devastating outcomes for organizations that find themselves facing difficult times.

When preparing for organizational change, leaders must consider the person-to-person interactions within their organizations. For larger enterprises, this adds multiple layers of concern when considering the impact that organizational change can have on its members collectively as well as individually. To address these issues, change leaders will need to focus on bridging the relationship between vision and action. This one step aligns thought and behavior so that organizational members are aware of the mission, purpose, and expected outcomes.

Another critical factor for organizational leaders to consider is determining the opportune time to make organizational changes. This means that leaders must assess organizational readiness by examining members' willingness to embrace change. In other words, leaders must gauge their employees' level of motivation and be prepared to unpack their current mindset. To do this, leaders may employ several strategies. These strategies may include providing data that reveals organizational performance versus performance needs based on market trends. Additionally, leaders will need to ensure their team can do what will be required of them once the changes occur. With this in mind, organizational members must also believe in their ability to successfully implement the desired changes. While employees must be willing to implement changes (change commitment) and also have the capacity to make these changes (change efficacy), it is also critically important for employees to see the value that organizational change offers. This essential element helps shape the organizational culture needed to successfully persevere throughout the change process. Though organizational change readiness may increase the likelihood of positive results in some instances, in other instances it does not necessarily predict the outcome. This means that while an organization may be ready for change and is capable of implementing the required changes, it will not be successful if the plans are inadequate or poorly designed. When leaders consider these factors, it increases the potential for organizational change to have positive results. The change in individuals may be accredited to Organizational Citizenship Behavior (OCB). With this change, an individual becomes motivated to perform as an individual as well as a contributing member of the team. This motivation allows the individual to be both innovative and creative to increase overall performance. The idea of OCB aligns with the notion of employees becoming psychologically empowered to change. While the motivation for this change may be relative to personal achievement, it counterintuitively works in the organization's favor. Regardless of the reason for the motivation, change leaders can benefit from the changed attitudes and commitment to go through the change process.

Innovation and Growth

Businesses vary according to the size of the company, the number of employees, and even the product or service the business provides. However, one aspect that is common among most businesses, regardless of its size or number of years in business, is the need to grow and expand. This requires leadership with the capacity to steer organizational goals while also deploying efforts to continually grow the business. To accomplish this, business leaders must maintain the necessary skill sets to sustain the business yet be capable of expanding products, services, and even the organization. For new startups, it may take several years of trying and many failures before entrepreneurs can achieve success or begin receiving a return on investment. When attempting to accomplish organizational goals, companies utilize various strategies. Regardless of the industry or size of the organization, there is a need to sustain the business as well as maintain a slight advantage over the competition. Entrepreneurial expert Eric Ries postulates that entrepreneurship is a kind of management (2011, p. 21). When considering a new venture, one must view the dichotomy of being an entrepreneur and managing a business through the same lens. From this perspective, leaders can begin with a new idea then use the same passion and innovation to continue building a thriving business. To enjoy the success of a new venture then benefit from a flourishing business, entrepreneurs must expect and learn from previous mistakes.

One of the common mistakes made by entrepreneurs is maintaining a narrow focus. Too often the primary focus is on product development. It makes sense that time and effort are spent creating and developing the product. After beginning to bring their dream to fruition, an entrepreneur eats, sleeps, and breathes that dream. Understandably, it could be easy to lose sight of the other important factors which are necessary for business development. Entrepreneurial expert Eric Ries asserts that business development entails more than just developing the product. He contends that considerations must be given to customer development (Ries, 2011). While developing a business, entrepreneurs benefit when they determine who their core customers will likely be and then develop a plan to ensure that they get the business of those potential customers. Another common mistake is failing to further develop a product, expand services, or increase the list of potential clients. To ensure the product will sustain the market as well as be able to maintain an edge over its competitors, it is also critical for new entrepreneurs to ensure they have a viable and unique product. Having a product that allows your business to stand out amongst competitors is a wise strategy. Further strategic measures entail having the capacity to build upon the product and take it to another level. Startup expert Guy Kawasaki agrees and refers to this as having a business plan (2004, p. 80). The development of a business plan merges both the product and a customer base.

The desire to innovate can occur with independent entrepreneurs as well as with those who are already a part of an organization and inspiring to creatively add to the business. Like entrepreneurs, innovators are creative beings with new ideas. Innovation expert Gary Oster describes innovation as a process through which the intentional development of a product or service is derived (2011, p. 3). The desire to create typically begins with an idea that helps to solve an issue or to improve upon things already in existence. Regardless of whether a new entrepreneur is wanting to develop a new startup, or an individual is bringing innovation to an existing business, what matters most is the fact that they can get started. Kawasaki mentions that while these are two distinct starting points for individual entrepreneurs and current workers looking to expand the business, each is certain to face challenges. The one certain thing is that both will face challenges, though the challenges will differ (Kawasaki, 2004, p. 80). Persistence is one of the tools that will assist entrepreneurs and innovators with pushing through the challenges. However, for many entrepreneurs, the issue is not sticking to the idea of starting a business but first coming up with a plan to bring the idea to fruition. Kawasaki, in his work The Art of the Start, reveals another tool that may be beneficial. This tool for success is utilizing a business model that has already been tried and proven (p. 80). In other words, a key factor for business success is finding a model that works and then nurturing its development. Time has proven that following a successful business plan is an effective method. The success of Starbucks, for example, is the result of the leader developing an effective business plan. Leadership experts Schultz and Yang credit Starbucks corporation's success to their business model along with the company's long-standing values which draw customers regardless of the distance, competition, or even cultural practices. Oftentimes, businesses start with just an idea. The ability to take an idea and turn it into a business requires work and dedication but most importantly, a plan. Entrepreneurs must employ key strategies to develop and further grow their business. Key strategies include using a business model to help steer the product as well as the process while making certain to communicate the plan.

There are many effective strategies for entrepreneurs seeking to start new ventures. While planning takes place at the beginning phases of business development, it is also an ongoing process. With this in mind, entrepreneurs are able to begin with a well-designed plan then continue monitoring and managing the business as it grows and develops. Although an entrepreneur may have a written plan which is communicated then analyzed to test for strengths, weaknesses, opportunities, and threats, it does not necessarily mean the plan will be foolproof. The value that a new product, idea, or service adds to the community or an existing business is intensified by its developer's passion and purpose. Essentially, the future success of organizations is only as good as the ideas and the people who create these new concepts. When leaders place themselves at the center of their business plan (Snyder & Duarte, 2008), the business development process can be smoothly integrated as part of business operations (p. 25). This requires the cooperation and collaboration of workers across all levels within the organization (p. 26). Ultimately, this will help organizations drive innovation and the success of the business. To ensure productivity, businesses rely on a dual approach formed of both rational and emotional contexts. This innovation dyad is the catalyst for success and builds on computer-aided assistance, referred to as the "innovation machine" (p.60) to generate ideas. Though innovation needs to be embedded in organizations as a part of their strategic plans for continual growth, organizational leaders must ensure innovation as well as productivity to achieve success (p. 43). This strategy can work well for organizations when leaders share their vision and provide guidance throughout the innovation and change process (p. 59). While it all begins with an idea, the capacity to develop strategies along with a business plan helps to achieve the intended goals for business leaders. During this process, business leaders should expect to make mistakes along the way. However, those mistakes will be lessons in which to learn from and grow.

As the world evolves, it becomes increasingly important for companies to continuously innovate and grow. As mentioned previously, Starbucks is one such company that has increasingly developed. The company has mastered the art of directing efforts toward customer satisfaction and building marketing strategies that target specific customers. Leaders at Starbucks (Schultz & Yang, 1997), recognize the importance of remaining authentic to maintain the reputation the corporation has established yet continuously innovating for further growth (p. 226). These aspects, along with the long-standing values of the company has generated success. Leaders of Starbucks Corporation were able to observe this first-hand through one of its international locations. At the grand opening of the Tokyo location, customers crowded the store in a continuous flow and, despite customary beliefs, did not mind purchasing beverages to go. While growth and success have been two sides of the same coin for Starbucks, some companies face challenges when attempting to make changes.

A challenge for most leaders is understanding exactly what changes need to occur and how to implement those changes. Though innovation disrupts the status quo, it is a necessary strategy for organizational leaders. Innovation experts Rindova & Petkova (2007) emphasize, due to technological advances, innovation adds value to businesses, particularly as the world evolves (p. 217). From this perspective, innovation is viewed as both necessary and good. However, due to uncertainties, many leaders are hesitant when deciding whether to make organizational changes. As leaders are reminded of the grace they have been extended, they are able to allow their creativity to merge with the Divine Creator's favor. With this in mind, Christian leaders should become exploratory in their innovative efforts. In other words, leaders should not be afraid to get radical. Radical innovation requires leaders who are unafraid to explore and experiment. Exploration is a key strategy that becomes reinforced when leaders are aware of God's presence throughout the organizational change process. This is a distinction observed between those who are called to lead versus those who are not. While many challenges exist for leaders when considering whether to make organizational changes, today's Christian leaders can transform their organizations when using Scripture as a guide.

Organizational change is necessary and can be successful but not often without its set of challenges. While processes are implemented to ensure efficiency, it does not account for unpredictable factors, such as human behavior and unintended outcomes. For this reason, organizations may not obtain the intended results after making changes. Though change leaders are visionaries and can see the benefits of changing the mission of an organization, the employees often observe change as something that is complex and disruptive to the organization. When this occurs, it typically reveals a concern that many organizations are faced with: changing the culture.

Organizational Culture

A challenge for many leaders is the ability to create an atmosphere where workers feel comfortable sharing their ideas or concerns. Inversely, it is expressed that followers face the same challenge regardless of whether or not the culture allows for such feedback. Does the culture determine the effectiveness of the leader's power? Is effective leadership synonymous with power? Criticism exists for leaders who are considered tough and task-driven. From this perspective, the belief is that coercion, or fear, is the driving force by which followers are led to fulfill goals. Most would agree that a certain level of fear is unavoidable, or even warranted at certain times. For example, a leader may choose to address unfavorable employee performance or behavior through written corrective action measures to deter undesirable behaviors or performance. However, while one leader may deem this tactic as extreme, another may view this course of action as necessary. Would forceful leadership be considered ineffective? Critics exist on both sides of the spectrum. Those who believe that force is necessary for leadership power supports the notion that force is an essential tool to operate and contend without force, leadership is weakened.

Leaders, while managing employees, processes, and products, also strive to create a culture with shared espoused values. Culture expert Edgar Schein (2010) notes that the creation of culture derives from three main sources: the values and beliefs of founding members, learning through experiences, and new values, beliefs, and assumptions of new organizational leaders and members (p. 219). For leaders to effectively lead and manage their organizations, leaders must develop a dynamic paradoxical balance (Cameron & Quinn, 2011, p. 53). Otherwise, cultural incongruence can create discord that is reflected in employee morale, behavior, and performance (p.85). When this occurs, the organizational climate is impacted by behaviors that contradict supposed organizational values. It is up to the leader to change the culture and strengthen the stability of the various subcultures so that everyone has the same shared assumptions to impact the organization as a whole. If the style and strength of the leader are in congruence with the organizational culture, both the leader and the organization will be successful (p. 52). When the leader's vision becomes shared assumptions, therein lies stability, culture change, and a team that can work together towards organizational goals.

Though changes in the culture may be necessary, it can be a difficult task to change either group members or individual behavior. The culture of an organization has a significant impact on establishing a climate that fosters and nurtures how individual ethics and behaviors are formed. While establishing the culture, leaders must also ensure appropriate planning of the change process to avoid negatively impacting organizational change. Although it may be the leader's intention to maximize resources and expand the organization, their efforts could have an adverse effect. For example, instead of the intended results, the organizational change could cause low productivity, poor morale, and little to no job satisfaction for employees. For this reason, leaders must take an approach that carefully cultivates the desired culture.

Organizational culture is best described as a 3-tier approach defining the heart of an organization:

1. The First Step – Understanding organizational culture is to examine an organization at the surface or its artifacts. At first glance, when entering an organization, the physical infrastructure, the layout of the organization, and the behavior of employees is an instant method of understanding the climate under which an organization operates.

2. The Second Step – Understanding organizational culture is interacting with members within the organization to identify what they believe they are to do to meet the goals of the organizations, or shared values.

3. The Third Step – Basic underlying assumptions provides depth to the logic of the shared assumptions. For example, the success of certain processes, when repeated and consistently successful, develops an underlying assumption the process is tried and true, and therefore, the only solution.

(Schein, 2010, p. 23.)

Leaders face challenges of cultivating cultures across multi-generations. Organizations across the country have operated for many years with gaps that span over three to four generations. Future predictions indicate that the workplace would eventually consist of five generations (Shah, 2011). For this reason, leaders are challenged with recruiting and managing workers that would merge with the existing culture while maintaining a productive workforce. To prepare for the multigenerational workforce of the future, leaders must have the foresight and take initiative to address the issues that may result from diverse populations. The demographics of the diverse populations include Traditionalists, Baby Boomers, Generation X, Millennials and Generation Z. These demographics provide a general description of the age range and depict typical behaviors. However, demographics provide a global view of specific eras but do not account for individual situations.

Cultivating the culture of an organization is a necessary task for leaders. It is often 'after the fact' that company executives find out about unhappy workers. At this point, there has either been a mass exodus or employee morale has severely suffered, resulting in a toxic environment. Research shows that workers leave when they feel the environment is unsupportive and punitive, there is insufficient recognition or appreciation, or there is a lack of opportunity for growth. Inversely, many organizational leaders find that employees remain with the company if they deem the organization a good fit, where the employee feels as if the relationship is mutually beneficial. Employees are also inclined to remain at an organization when the leader provides both emotional and task-related support, and when there is a positive climate. Successful leaders can recognize toxic cultures and develop solutions to address employee concerns.

Possible solutions to increase overall efficiency, address employee concerns, and continue to develop as an organization include forming a partnership with a consultant. This consideration can determine long-term solutions for existing challenges. Hiring a consultant is key for today's leaders to be proactive about seeking ways to become innovative while maintaining sustainability. Ultimately, consulting creates opportunities for organizations to maintain a culture that aligns with the values which drive the organizational mission. Organizational leaders possess a high level of responsibility when attempting to maintain a business. Besides economic concerns, high turnover rates can result in worker burnout for those who remain and, ultimately, impact productivity. Unfortunately, this could result in dire consequences for the business. However, resolutions to decrease attrition rates and increase overall efficiency can help leaders continue to move their organization in the right direction.

Data-Driven Organizations

When organizational leaders fail to use data as a basis for making decisions, there is a gap in understanding the value that data-driven decisions allow. Big data is best explained as not only offering information to corporations but gaining a deeper understanding of the business and taking a high-level approach to solving critical issues. This may be presented in the form of new initiatives, products, or services based on an analysis of changes in patterns (Davenport, Barth, & Bean, 2012). In the health industry, for example, data analytics can be useful in determining the best treatments for patients as well as cures for certain diseases. When leaders begin to understand the benefits of using data analytics, they must next determine the organizational structure that will be best for the business.

The use of social networks has become widespread across many business sectors as well as government and health organizations. As the utilization of social media becomes more prevalent, so does its reliance. Therefore, businesses seek to garner an innovative and structured way of collecting and storing data. These efforts, data mining techniques, can be extrapolated into spreadsheets or other graphics to include charts and graphs (Injadat, Salo, & Nassif, 2016). While spreadsheets are widely used, it also has some limitations. For example, data may automatically be computed as zero for missing cells (Savage, Zhang, Yu, Chou, & Wang, 2014), ultimately changing statistical results. For this reason, due to its lack of reliability, spreadsheets cannot replace statistical software without financial and other implications. In addition to the validity of spreadsheets, information from social network sources could be unreliable as well. Research indicates that information can be skewed due to the work of computer hackers, spammers, and other online predators (Savage, Zhang, Yu, Chou, & Wang, 2014). These anomalies also impact the validity of data retrieved from social media.

While some data collection methods have its drawbacks, the use of business analytics are critical for organizational growth and development. Adapting and maintaining a data-driven culture, requires more than 'business as usual'. To implement this effectively, business leaders should be aware of the key players, have an understanding of the individual roles that each play, then strategically place data practitioners throughout the company. Investors, consumers, practitioners, and directors all play an integral part in the capability of organizations to make data-driven decisions. The most significant role is that of data practitioners, who are responsible for using data to solve problems within the organizations (Bartlett, 2013). Data practitioners are highly skilled and well-educated individuals that add value to organizations. In these roles, data practitioners familiarize themselves with the business without becoming too familiar with the workers to gain a thorough understanding of business operations. Scripture reminds us that, "An intelligent heart acquires knowledge, and the ear of the wise seeks knowledge" (Proverbs 18:15). With a quantitative academic background as well as advanced academic and post-graduate work, data practitioners are excellent resources for the workplace and its workers.

Leaders also have several options to consider when determining how to spread data analysts throughout the organization. One option for analyst groups is maintaining a centralized structure where analysts, who may be housed at the corporate office, report directly to corporate leadership while working on various projects as assigned by the organization's leader

(Davenport, Harris, & Morison, 2010). Using the Consulting Model, supervisors can bring in analysts to address issues in their particular units. This approach used by both United Airlines and eBay focus on remaining competitive within the industry. The Functional Model allows analysts to operate as part of a unit while addressing issues specific to that unit while also consulting with other departments at the same time. While the Center of Excellence (COE) Model provides a sense of community and comradery for analysts who are strategically placed within every major unit of the organization, the Decentralized Model is a fragmented approach that is highly ineffective (Davenport, Harris, & Morison, 2010).

When seeking to hire data analysts, organizational leaders must remain diligent yet flexible. While business leaders use traditional methods for recruiting and hiring analysts, one of the most advantageous strategies in recruiting analysts is forging a partnership with universities well known for their academic rigor. Additionally, organizational leaders should continually draw on available resources. While companies seek to hire analysts externally, leaders may have to consider taking advantage of skill sets of existing employees. Other strategies include seeking analysts locally as well as globally.

Due to an increasing number of data-driven senior managers and advanced technology, along with information overload, organizations find themselves having to maintain a competitive edge by adopting new processes. This means that corporations must conduct research, analyze data, and develop a structure to apply what they have learned. Therefore, corporations must first be capable of handling a stream of information. Second, they must be able to both analyze and determine the value of the data. Third, corporations will have to ensure they are appropriately staffed and operate efficiently to perform successfully.

In the retail industry, for example, strategies to identify key customers is critical for business. Keeping track of customers that spend the most money and most frequently is need-to-know information for retail management. Conversely, it is beneficial to monitor those who frequently return merchandise. While frequent shoppers help retail businesses thrive, costs incurred by serial returners can be damaging for business (Davenport, Harris, & Morison, 2010).

When determining how to best collect, store, and analyze data, those in the retail industry are not only able to track patterns of behavior but monitor customer preferences as well. For example, Netflix is a revolutionary approach to selecting movies that afford customers the convenience of ordering movies online (Davenport, Harris, & Morison, 2010). This demonstrates what can occur when the right data is filtered through the right resources.

To effectively integrate business analytics, leaders must consider critical elements. One of the most essential factors to be evaluated is potential risks. Though there may be some advantages to corporations using business analytics, organizational leaders should be careful to avoid making erroneous decisions. TransAlta, a Canadian based firm, is noted as making a documentation error that costed the company to lose contractual work worth $24MM (Davenport, Harris, & Morison, 2010, p. 12). Mistakes of this magnitude can be linked to two areas: logic errors and process errors. NASA found this out the hard way after making a costly decision based on assumptions that were not relevant or tested (Davenport, Harris, & Morison, 2010, p. 12). Logic errors occur when organizations fail to ask pertinent questions or develop faulty assumptions plus fail to put the assumption to the test. Process errors will occur due to systemic issues such as careless mistakes and bad decision making by leaders. Organizations will be able to use Big Data effectively at the convergence of information technology and business analytics (Bartlett, 2013, p. 4). Business analytics has become widespread due to the growth and expansion of new software applications (Bartlett, 2013). With this development, companies across various industries can recognize the value in tracking, monitoring, and analyzing data. A key strategy for leaders is focusing on information that enhances the organization's distinctive capabilities. When this occurs, it allows companies to develop a unique business model to achieve success while providing customers with an optimal experience. This is driven by the identification of analytical targets and the use of this information advantageously. The focus of data analytics significantly impacts the decision-making process for leaders. When leaders consider analytical targets, they can remain competitive.

DISCUSSION QUESTIONS

1. What roadblocks exist within your organization that is preventing organizational growth?

2. Which strategies have proven to be most effective to address those barriers?

3. What opportunities exist for your organization's growth?

4. How will you allow data to impact decision-making and innovation for your company?

THE HEART OF AN ORGANIZATION

"If you want to know why your people are not performing well, step up to the mirror and take a peek."
~Kenneth H. Blanchard

One of the vital organs in the body is that of the heart. Analogously, a leader is to an organization what the heart is to the body. From this perspective, the leader is critical to the functioning of the organization and integral in steering its mission towards intended goals. Essentially, the leader is the heartbeat of the organization. This means that leadership is a critical component to which followers depend and, at the same time, a leader provides the necessary support for the team to function. As vital as the leader is to the organization, just as important as the leader's heart and his impact on followers.

Situational Leadership Theory

The leader-follower relationship determines both the climate and the productivity of an organization. The significance of this pivotal aspect can be measured by performance outcomes seen within organizations. While leadership styles will vary, the leadership style of the leader may also change depending on the situation. This is best described in the Situational Leadership Theory. The Situational Leadership Theory is observed as a particular style of leadership in which the leader adapts his or her style according to the demands of the organization or any particular situation that arises (Northouse, 2013, p. 99). This two-dimensional style focuses on leaders being able to either give directives or be supportive, depending on the situation. Successful situational leaders are those who are able to identify the strengths and needs of their workers and then adjust their leadership style to the individual worker. For this reason, to be effective, situational leaders must know their subordinates and be aware of changes in their behaviors. This dynamic can have a significant impact on the leader-follower relationship and directly influence employee performance. The follower's perception of the leader further reinforces the influence leaders have on their followers. This becomes increasingly important as technology advances and companies expand across countries. Is the success of global enterprises significantly dependent upon their followers? The answer to that question is yes. Globalization best describes a current state of affairs whereby the events and actions or people and governments around the world have become interdependent. Leaders and followers are inter-dependent upon one another to maintain cohesiveness as a team.

Team Leadership Model

The Team Leadership Model explains the team concept as fundamental to an organization's overall success. This model, also referred to as the Hill Model, focuses on the functional leader approach which views the leader as having the capacity to function as needed to operate efficiently and effectively. Hill's Model for Team Leadership identifies both internal and external leadership actions (Northouse, 2013). Depending on the circumstance, the two leadership actions will be followed by certain necessary interventions: task, relational, or environmental. Task-oriented intervention includes goal focusing, structuring for results, facilitating decisions, training, and maintaining standards. Relational intervention includes: coaching, collaborating, managing conflict, building commitment, satisfying needs, and modeling principles. Environmental intervention includes: networking, advocating, negotiating support, buffering, assessing, and sharing information. The type of intervention a leader determines to be necessary for the follower will be dependent upon the situation. The chosen method of intervention for team members must be carefully decided for the continuity of team effectiveness (p. 290). A sports reference, to bring this into context, is a coach continually pushing players to play their hardest and continue winning games despite the fact the team is on a winning streak. The future success of the team remains as important as the current winning status. This is synonymous with leaders and coaches building teams that focus on remaining efficient rather than simply celebrating past successes. Though the Team Leadership Model works to improve leader-follower relationships by using a team approach for organizational effectiveness, there are also cons to this approach. The approach can create disorder, causing the organization to operate inefficiently.

Leader-Follower Relationship

When there is dysfunction in the organization, the intended purpose of the team leadership model is defunct. This dysfunction results in a lack of unity amongst the team along with a diminished sense of purpose. When this occurs, it has a direct impact on the success of the organization as well as the leader-follower relationship. Therefore, to perform as a team, the leader-follower relationship must maintain authenticity and integrity. Both the leader and the follower share the responsibility and are accountable for the organization's success. Historical contexts presume that followership is as important as leadership. Accordingly, egocentrism should be void of the leader's style to further maintain the leader-follower relationship. Integrity within organizations begins with the leader and reveals the values that are important to him or her. Business experts John Mackey and Raj Sisodia point out the primary focus for leaders should be on the customers, shareholders, and employees (Mackey & Sisodia, 2013, p. 10). When the shifts changes for the leader and the focus is on people, the economic gain will follow. Leaders who are cognizant of this have an alignment between their heads and their hearts and are consciously aware that they can accomplish tasks because of their team.

Exemplary Practices of Leadership

Certain behaviors are characteristic of effective leaders. Leadership experts James M. Kouzes & Barry Posner (2012) identify five attributes as exemplary leadership practices. The Five Practices of Exemplary Leadership that assist in creating shared culture include: *Modeling the Way; Inspiring a Shared Vision; Challenging the Process; Enabling Others to Act;* and *Encouraging the Heart*.

Modeling the Way

Modeling behavior expected of followers is considered to be more effective than merely telling followers what's expected. Leaders need to practice what they preach. They must ensure their actions are consistent with their words.

Inspiring Shared Vision

Forward-thinking leaders and those who are visionaries are usually highly effective. Exemplary leaders can envision the future of their organization, including all possible futures, and share that vision with their team. Leaders who articulate their values and model intended behavior can inspire others to follow.

Challenging the Process

Leaders should create an atmosphere where workers are encouraged to ask questions. When workers feel like valued members of the team, they will offer solutions and provide input that proves valuable to the organization.

<u>Enabling Others to Act</u>

Today's leaders should seek to empower their followers. The need exists for leaders who are concerned with developing more leaders versus their selfish gains.

<u>Encouraging the Heart</u>

Organizations must remain creative in how they recognize individuals for their work. Due to budget constraints, intrinsic rewards are more commonplace than extrinsic rewards. Leadership experts point out that recognition is one of the most valuable rewards that employers could provide that bears no cost for the organization.

For an organization to run smoothly and effectively, leaders must depend on the workers. At the same time, when organizations use incentives, this helps motivate employee behavior. In other words, employee behavior and performance can be controlled by incentives (p. 17).

Leaders who are in the position to empower and elevate future leaders must first engage with those they are attempting to lead. Empowering workers offers encouragement and promotes energy that allows them to thrive. Part of this process involves having an open-door policy. An open-door policy allows workers to be aware that the leader is approachable and makes time for important things. When leaders are approachable, this establishes a climate of trust that allows for open communication. Leadership experts view effective communication as a necessary tool that fosters collaboration and perpetuates organizational success.

An illustration of effective leadership through communication and collaboration is seen on one of television's premier reality shows, *Undercover Boss*. The show features leaders who go undercover, in disguise, to avoid being recognized by their employees. The idea behind this experiment is to get a glimpse of internal operations at various locations, gain insight about employees' attitudes or thoughts about the company, and learn what they can do to improve. While participation in this show allows leaders to learn more about their company from the outside looking in, it also requires a level of vulnerability and transparency for organizational leaders. Some of the companies represented on the *Undercover Boss* television show include executives from NASCAR, Choice Hotels, DirecTV, Great Wolf Lodge, and Herschend Family Entertainment. The show demonstrates leadership values that are revealed as the executives learn then take action to resolve issues and address concerns based on feedback obtained from employees. It further reveals the leadership characteristic found to be one of the most endearing parts of the show: compassion. At the end of the show, the executives reveal themselves to workers they have come into contact with while disguised. At this point, the executives inform workers about the impact made during their interactions. The executives then, typically, award some sort of financial compensation, charitable donation, or scholarship to those employees who the CEO has come into contact with and may be facing challenges, are deserving of recognition, or need additional support. This level of love and compassion enhances the worker's perception of the leader as well as their belief in the organization. Ultimately, the leader-follower relationship is strengthened and job satisfaction along with performance is increased. This CBS hit television show depicts leadership qualities workers describe as respectful, cooperative, joyful, and loving. In other words, leaders who lead with love appear to be most effective.

Love is at the core of leadership. There is a direct correlation between effective leadership and a positive spirit of leadership that is demonstrated when interacting with followers. Successful leaders are those capable of leading by treating internal and external customers well. While leading with love is considered counterintuitive, its absence can breed a toxic environment. Scripture reminds us in Ephesians 4:32 leaders are to "Be ye kind to one another, tenderhearted, forgiving one another, even as God for Christ's sake hath forgiven you." Success as a leader involves being able to lead with compassion, a forgiving heart, and empathy.

Likewise, at the core of leadership is the leader's ability to communicate. When organizational leaders develop active listening and critical thinking skills, it sets them apart to be able to receive and decode verbal, nonverbal, and para-verbal communication of followers regardless of any barriers. The established communication between leaders and followers deemed as effective is referred to as participative management. Research shows emotional intelligence, a key leadership trait, as being central in the participative management process (Ruderman, Hannum, Leslie, & Steed, 2001, p. 3). Emotional intelligence is observed as the ability of leaders to be keenly aware of and in control of their own emotions while also being cognizant of another person's emotions to work toward a common goal (Ruderman et al., 2001, p. 3). A leader's ability to predict a followers' responses is critical when attempting to gain buy-in and requires leaders to engage employees throughout the decision-making process. This is the essence of participative management. From this perspective, emotional intelligence highlights strengths within leaders which are demonstrated through the leader's actions. Leaders with a high level of emotional intelligence can effectively communicate by engaging others as well as making them feel at ease, relaxed, and comfortable in their presence.

John Wooden, who was recognized for having won the most NCAA championships in basketball history, was the epitome of leading with love and being a great communicator. Mr. Wooden prided himself on the fact that his teams were able to 'outperform and outlast' their competitors. As a coach, Mr. Wooden believed in more than just the game. While he cared about the success of the team and organization, he had a greater love for making an impact on the lives of his players. For that reason, he taught about more than just basketball. Mr. Wooden was known for teaching his players and others about life. John Wooden's philosophies are found in his published work, The Pyramid of Success. Through his work, he identifies several key characteristics that leaders must maintain when leading others (Wooden, 2009). When the leadership style of the leader is consistent with his or her values and it becomes aligned with the experiences of followers (Schein, 2010, p. 219), the organization can operate efficiently while continuing to grow.

Many examples exist of exceptional leaders with values that have had long-lasting impact on employees as well as their performance. One such example of an extraordinary leader is General Colin Powell. General Powell, during his military career and political appointments, demonstrated high levels of emotional intelligence and modeled behavior that was expected of his followers. He demonstrated the qualities that leadership experts, Duval & Hayes (2012) identify as necessary for leaders. Those qualities include being "honest, forward-looking, competent, and inspiring" (p. 36). When a leader's leadership style is guided with values in mind, leaders can effectively inspire followers to accomplish goals. In other words, these characteristics are indicative of who they are and not what they do (Duvall & Hays, 2012, p. 36). Self-awareness, then, is essential for leadership development.

There are many leadership attributes which guides the leader's actions. Virtuous leaders are led by habits of both the heart and the mind. One of the cardinal virtues that drive behavior is wisdom. Wisdom is considered to be the master virtue that allows leaders to use good judgment, be decisive, and discern correctly. This comes with both maturity as well as a change in mindset. In other words, leaders must work towards being humble and wise through spiritual development. When that occurs, newfound wisdom provides a sense of clarity and focus that affects the heart and spirit. When Christian leaders do as the Apostle Paul suggests in Philippians 3:12-14, to "press on toward the goal of the prize for the upward call of God in Christ Jesus", they allow themselves to be led by the Holy Spirit and can nurture their values.

Authentic Leadership

Wise leadership is reflective of Authentic Leadership, which is based on faith in leadership and is first seeded by the leaders' character. "A wise man has great power, and a man of knowledge increases strength" (Proverbs 24:5). Christian leaders can influence followers when leaders' values are demonstrated through their behaviors. This means appealing to the very core of Christians: their values and beliefs. This is in alignment with Scripture as revealed in I John that the actions of those who believed in God's Word demonstrated their belief by exercising their faith. The Christian community was encouraged by the Apostle John to live according to the Word which was in them and to refute worldly things. A further examination of the New Testament reveals innovative ways leaders appeal to followers. In the Apostle Paul's letters, he appeals to the people of Philippi to remain obedient to the Word and to remain strong in their faith. "Therefore, my beloved as you have always obeyed, so now, not only as in my presence but much more in my absence, work out your salvation with fear and trembling" (Philippians 2:12). From this perspective, those who follow God's commandment will reject resistance and be willing to do God's will to receive his promises.

Cognizance of one's personality traits help to define the person and, ultimately, the kind of leader they are or need to become. Self-awareness is critically important for leaders to be able to make a difference in their work, organization, and lives of their followers. The leadership style the leader possesses can have an impact on the organization and, ultimately, make a difference in the success of the organization. Leaders can use various tools to assess their leadership style, including an Authentic Leadership Self-Assessment. This assessment is used to assess a leader's level of authentic leadership by analyzing four main components: self-awareness; internalized moral perspective; balanced processing; and relational transparency (Northouse, 2013, p. 281). A meta-analysis of various leaders conducted between 1967 and 1998 revealed five personality traits amongst leaders:

Big Five Personality Factors

1. Neuroticism - The tendency to be depressed, anxious, insecure, vulnerable, and hostile.
2. Extraversion - The tendency to be sociable and assertive and to have positive energy.

3. Openness - The tendency to be informed, creative, insightful, and curious.
4. Agreeableness - The tendency to be accepting, conforming, trusting, and nurturing.
5. Conscientiousness - The tendency to be thorough, organized, controlled, dependable, and decisive.

(Northouse, 2013, p. 27)

When evaluating the effectiveness of leaders, one's personality traits become a significant factor. Results from the study conducted strongly suggest that leaders who are extraverts are the most effective leaders followed by those leaders with conscientiousness, openness, and low neuroticism.

Transformational Leadership

Transformational Leadership is observed as a style of leadership whereby the leader engages with others to create a connection, that establishes a level of trust, allowing both the leader and the follower to be motivated (Northouse, 2013, p. 186). Transformational leadership is further described as being concerned with the professional development of their followers and working to develop followers to become the best versions of themselves. This awareness of followers provides insight for leaders to develop professional development plans for followers that align with the organization's missions while empowering workers as well. Transformational leadership explicates the style of leadership necessary for organizational design and structural changes. Leaders who wish to influence and have strong moral values are capable of changing the culture of a corporate environment to one that is more humane and less regimented. Developing transformational leaders to have a servanthood mentality is tantamount to how Christian leaders can align their agenda with God's agenda while promoting unity and cohesiveness in the cultures and followers they lead. Espousing a servanthood mentality will allow Christian leaders to effectively transform their organizations.

Transactional Leadership

Transactional Leadership is described as a style that fosters an exchange between leaders and their followers (Northouse, 2013, p. 186). This is seen, for example, during political campaigns when various candidates announce their platforms. An exchange between politicians and constituents occurs as the politician makes promises about policies and actions that will take place once they are in office. In turn, there is a level of trust and belief garnered, causing the constituent to want to vote for this particular candidate. This particular style of leadership is seen in many situations to include all industries and on various levels.

Path-Goal Theory

The Path-Goal Theory places emphasis on the correlation between the leadership style of those who lead, the individual behavior of followers, and the work environment as a whole. This means that workers are motivated by the belief that their efforts will result in something worthwhile. In other words, employees are encouraged when they are confident in their abilities to perform their duties and will be recognized or rewarded for their work. Scholars view the payoffs as a means of motivation for workers, particularly if the payoffs are monetary awards. In a changing economy, however, it is not always possible for leaders to reward employees monetarily. Ultimately, the responsibility lies on the leader to motivate employees toward completing their work. To accomplish this, leaders must adapt their style according to the needs of their subordinates as each follower brings an individual set of characteristics to the work environment. Ultimately, the end goal is achieving the overall goals for the organization as a team versus rewarding individual contributions. The theory holds that the leader variably interchanges some or all of the behaviors depending on the situation and the motivational needs of subordinates.

The four types of leader behaviors include:

1. Directive Leadership – The leader provides subordinates with instructions to include expectations and performance standards which are made clear to all.
2. Supportive Leadership – The leader is attentive to the well-being and needs of the subordinates, treating each of them as if they are equals.
3. Participative Leadership – The leader includes subordinates in the decision-making by consulting with them and gathering their insight about how things should function.
4. Achievement-Oriented Leadership – The leader sets high standards of excellence while challenging subordinates to continuously improve.

(Northouse, 2013, p.140)

Servant Leadership

In Philippians 2, Paul "lets his light shine" as Jesus' servant leader. He demonstrates a basis for allowing leaders to lead for the benefit of others. This is relevant for today's leaders. Paul's love for Christ and his servant-leader style shares similar characteristics of transformational leadership. This dyad is reflective of how contemporary leaders should lead, having Christ-like character at all times.

When leading globally, leaders must maintain certain characteristics to lead successfully. Leading cross-culturally also requires key competencies such as the ability to communicate effectively (Lingenfelter, 2008). While communication is an essential aspect, leaders must also be capable of building trust as well as developing a sense of community. With this in mind, leaders should focus on leading so that Christ is exemplified. For example, when faced with tough decisions in times of crisis, leaders who prioritize love for God's people over personal comforts clearly show what love, humility, and empathy means. When followers observe leaders showing their love for Christ through their actions, this not only demonstrates for followers how they should lead but it also glorifies the ultimate leader, Jesus Christ.

From a Sociological Perspective

Scholars persist in further developing theories by analyzing the function and patterns of leaders. From a sociological orientation perspective, it is vital to gain an understanding of leadership to further catalyze a framework for change. In other words, leaders can become change agents, bringing order when and where it is necessary. Extraordinary leaders can create social order, ultimately changing the culture of the organization to complete the mission. To effectively achieve the mission of organizations, leaders must consider their most important resources: the workers. Organizational leaders must also ensure that workers share the same espoused values as their leader. The leader sets the tone by embedding the mission and the culture of the organization, inevitably creating the ability to develop and cultivate a team. By doing this, leaders can shape the employees' behaviors as they seek to fit into the culture of the organization. The connection between one's heart and one's virtues helps to drive one's behavior. Scholars identify the heart as the defining object that allows one person's conduct to be different from that of another, which shifts the mind and focus to do as Christ would do (Faulhaber, 2008, p, 129). In essence, the only difference between one man's fate and that of another is what is in his heart. Some scholars would argue that love is not just an emotion. The virtue of love is a will that prompts behavior, or for one to act. Therefore, what is in the heart is the basis for one's actions. As a Christian leader, love for God and desire to please Him becomes the motivation that guides one to live righteously. In other words, those who are moved by God are filled with a desire in their heart, mind, and soul to act and do as they are moved by God to do.

A resonating theme throughout the second chapter of Philippians is the many examples of servant leadership displayed throughout scripture. Servant leadership as presented is reflective of a way to bring about positivity in a changing world. Though servant leadership and transformational leadership are not competing leadership styles, there are many more similarities between the two than there are differences. Transformational leadership is concerned with values and ethics that sets the standard to achieve long-term goals. Transformational leadership promotes engagement between leaders and followers that drive morality and motivation for both the leader and the follower. Some of the world's greatest leaders like Dr. Martin Luther King, Abraham Lincoln, Mahatma Gandhi, Mother Theresa, and Nelson Mandela have been identified as servant leaders. Other great leaders such as President Barack Obama and Hilary Clinton have been called transformational leaders. The ultimate leader, Jesus Christ, is the greatest of all transformational leaders. Under this leadership style, leaders operate as role models for followers, to demonstrate the values they wish for followers to adopt. Transformational leadership explicates the style of leadership necessary to implement organizational design and structure changes. Leaders who wish to influence and have strong moral values are capable of obtaining these objectives. Further understanding of the transformational leadership theory relates the relationship between leader and follower and the exchange that allows for desired outcomes to be achieved.

DISCUSSION QUESTIONS

1. Which leadership theory explains your leadership style?

2. Who are the leaders that you identify with or have been inspired by?

3. How does your values align with the values of your organization?

HUMILITY IS MORE THAN JUST AN EIGHT LETTER WORD

"Being others-focused instead of self-focused changes your worldview. Living in a selfless manner and seeking to help others enriches your very existence on a daily basis. Get your hands dirty once in a while by serving in a capacity that is lower than your position or station in life. This keeps you tethered to the real world and grounded to reality, which should make it harder to be prideful and forget where you came from"
~ Miles Anthony Smith

There is a direct correlation between leadership and character. In other words, effective leaders are those who are capable of inspiring others based on who they are and not just what they do. Essentially, these leadership characteristics are motivators that help drive employee behavior. Key strategies for leaders to be successful in their leadership roles include leading with both the heart and mind. This requires leaders to nurture two cardinal virtues: humility and wisdom. Leadership expert Jim Collins refers to great leaders as individuals with personal humility having professional drive (p. 13). The story of Joshua reveals a follower who humbly serves, and ultimately, becomes a leader. Joshua, as an aide to Moses, is a faithful servant who can assume the leadership role and face challenges with confidence. Joshua had a drive even though he did not have the title of leader. Scholars agree that it does not matter who has the title, but those who have the heart of a servant and the drive of a leader. Two of the most defining characteristics of servant leaders are 1) The ability to influence others, and 2) Leading by example. This style of leadership is not only effective but indicative of the value of a leader which could ultimately transform society and solve world issues.

The following behaviors are identified as those embodied by servant leaders:

1. Conceptualizing
2. Emotional Healing
3. Putting Followers First
4. Helping Followers Grow and Succeed
5. Behaving Ethically
6. Empowering
7. Creating Value for the Community (Northouse, 2013)

When leaders can humble themselves by serving others as they seek to emulate the true servant, Jesus Christ, they set themselves apart and can achieve success.

EMPATHY: A LOST ART

"True compassion means not only feeling another's pain but also, being moved to help relieve it."
~Daniel Goleman

The late Kobe Bryant was an American National Basketball star who entered the league directly out of high school. While he held the position of shooting guard for the Los Angeles Lakers, Kobe was a star both on and off the court. After an outstanding 20-year career, Kobe retired. It was during an interview about his career, when Kobe was asked what advice he would give to basketball players beginning their careers in the basketball league. Kobe responded that he would offer compassion and empathy (Howes, 2018). His belief was, beyond any specialized skills, a leader needs to be unselfish and have good communication; but most importantly, a good leader needs to be compassionate and have empathy. Empathy is the ability to look through the lenses of someone else to understand what and how the individual may be feeling then responding accordingly. The ability to relate to another's feelings is at the core of who we are as human beings. From this perspective, having the mental capacity to understand another allows leaders to predict others' actions; leaders with this capacity possess a high level of emotional intelligence. Emotional intelligence is described as the ability of leaders to be keenly aware of and in control of their own emotions while also being cognizant of another person's emotions to appropriately respond (Ruderman et al., 2001, p. 3). From this perspective, emotional intelligence highlights strengths within leaders which are demonstrated through the leader's actions. Additionally, the leader must have the human factor and believe that people are intrinsically good. A positive outlook only reinforces the positive culture that leaders attempt to create. This basic belief will assist leaders with creating the culture and new leaders with affecting culture. Believing people are good and willing to work helps to design an organizational structure that promotes a sense of community and collaboration.

Fundamental Attribution Errors

Imagine getting up and starting your day only to step outside and realize that you have a flat tire. As you're about to walk back into the house to call roadside assistance, you realize that you have walked out of the house without your keys and you are now locked out of your house. Just as you are about to panic, you hear a bus coming down the street and realize that you can still make it to your job interview and deal with these issues later. You go into full sprint mode and make it to the bus just as the driver is closing the door. Maybe it's the look on your face, but the driver decides to open the door. You finally make it to the interview of that dream job you have been waiting for. You are 10 minutes late, but the receptionist tells you the manager will still see you. As you are walking past the receptionist, a whiff of air hits you and you realize that you did not have a chance to go to the bathroom to freshen up after your jog to the bus stop. Before the interview begins, you feel compelled to share the story about your morning. The manager determines that this disheveled person that arrived 10 minutes late and appeared as if they had just run a marathon was merely an irresponsible person with no regard for other people's time; the manager surmises that this must be typical of this person's character. This is an example of the Fundamental Attribution Error, which attributes a person's actions to their character, particularly depending on the other person's mood (Forgas, 1998, p. 318). Leaders who are empathetic and get to know their workers place value on the leader-follower relationship.

When leaders are cognizant of their workers' capabilities, they place themselves in a position to actively and continually build their teams to become more efficient. Teams function on a continuum that begins with a development of trust for the leader on behalf of the follower. As the trust builds, so does the resiliency to be able to handle challenges. The team shows growth when they are capable of a high level of interaction while managing conflicts. Subsequent growth occurs when the team buys into the mission of the organization and accepts accountability. At this interval, organizational leaders should be able to see the results of a team performing at an optimal level. Successful leaders will further understand the need to manage resources effectively. When organizational leaders maximize the strengths of their workers while managing their weaknesses (Stark, 2005), the necessary growth can occur while also meeting the needs of the organization. This alignment of the proper allocation of resources matched with clear expectations for the workers sets organizations apart from the competition. Effective leaders are those who are strategic thinkers and also follow the teachings in I Peter to use their gifts wisely. "As each has received a gift, use it to serve one another, as good stewards of God's varied grace" (I Peter 4:10). True servants are able to serve others just as Christ served the church.

AGILITY: HOW FLEXIBLE ARE YOU?

"Success today requires the agility and drive to constantly rethink, reinvigorate, react, and reinvent."
~Bill Gates

Organizations, regardless of their size, typically begin with a structure designed to meet the needs of the organization as it grows and develops. Organizations benefit from implementing a formal design that outlines specific tasks for each member of the organization. Therefore, whether formal or informal, organizations must have a plan to meet the goals of the organization. While organizational designs explain exactly who is responsible for doing what, it is strategically developed to drive the mission of an organization. The leader, when facilitating organizational design, must be decisive. However, this does not mean that once an organizational design is developed, it can never be redesigned.

Organizational design plays an integral role in helping businesses achieve their intended results. While work performance is influenced by leadership, organizational structure and design can have an even greater impact. Leadership expert, David Stehlik, posits that when cultural sensitivity aligns with the convergence of leadership and organizational design, organizations are on the path to being highly effective. An interruption in the status quo then would appear to do more harm than good. Agile leaders, however, are not only open to the possibility of innovation but rather deem it necessary. When deciding to innovate, managers must ensure that plans are in congruence with the size of the organization to sustain and grow. Due to factors such as economic growth, technology, and global expansion, existing organizational design may eventually become obsolete. When this occurs, organizations either innovate or consider organizational design solutions. There are many solutions for managers to consider when redesigning an organization.

Leaders must remain flexible and open to adjusting the organizational design as well as their style of leadership. This becomes critically important when leaders lead across cultures. When leaders understand and respect the differences of other cultures, customs, and religions, it enhances the leader's cultural agility. While leaders may never quite fit into different cultures, the transition becomes easier when leaders learn the history, respect the differences, and empathize with people from other cultures. These uncertainties can include political, environmental, and communication challenges that leaders must overcome.

It is key for leaders to be able to effectively deal with change. When leaders are agile, they set the example for followers to be able to adapt as well. When consultants remain agile and flexible, they can operate efficiently. Studies show that even the most well-designed plans may need to be adjusted. Despite having to adopt changes as part of organizational design, day-to-day operations should continue smoothly. Since change is viewed as a complex process, a change management project is required to successfully adapt to changes.

A change management project outlines a blueprint for effectively handling change. When using a change management project, the specified information is provided regarding specific details about the changes. This means that a systematic approach to change will occur by identifying specific changes, roles and responsibilities, and a timeline for the changes to occur. Organizational leaders must ensure a design strategy that is capable of integrating change projects while conducting business as usual.

When considering the future of an organization, leaders must take into account two of the most important elements of the organization: innovation and culture. Effective leaders can effectively craft the two together. Culture expert Edgar Schein (2010) postulates that culture and leaders are two sides of the same coin (p.22). While there is an ongoing debate about whether global leaders can transfer values when leading across various cultures, the success of the leader will be dependent upon the leader's character and capabilities. When leaders allow themselves to grow and develop, particularly in unfamiliar territory, this benefits the global leader as well as the business. Exemplifying a global mindset means possessing increased psychological, intellectual, and social capital. Not only will a global mindset add value to the leader but it will also add to the potential profit and worth of the company. Leaders who maintain a global mindset while exhibiting key cross-cultural competencies are an asset for any organization and will allow them to be successful when leading across cultures.

RESPONSIBILITY BEGINS
WITH THE LEADER

"Leadership involves the heavy burden of responsibility, and the fear of getting it wrong can paralyze a leader."
~ John C. Maxwell

O rganizational leaders bear the responsibility of leading people while managing processes and products. With these responsibilities come credit and accountability for successes as well as failures. However, the fear of getting it wrong should not paralyze a leader, nor should it cause their dreams to become stifled. Leaders have a responsibility to keep forging ahead and continue making strides to fulfill dreams or complete the mission of the organization. They must do this while being prepared for and expecting setbacks. While failed experiences present challenges it also allows for opportunities of learning and reinventing. A key strategy when working towards building success involves appropriately responding when things do not go quite as planned. Successful leaders are capable of learning from their mistakes then continuing to recreate, reinvent and further expand.

Researchers find leadership styles which causes anxiety creates an environment that decreases motivation, and ultimately, performance. The leadership styles of leaders play a major role in either increasing or reducing toxic levels within their organizations. Organizational leaders must be conscious of this and make every attempt to cultivate a sense of community within the work environment. The tone of the organization is set by the leader and becomes the bottom line for organizational success. Toxic behaviors such as micromanagement, personal vendettas, and extreme monitoring create a climate that is not conducive for productivity. Therefore, it is the responsibility of the leader to foster community and collaboration as a best practice for their organization.

Many decisions are made when structural changes are needed within an organization. Critical to the decision-making process is the ability of leaders to include workers by engaging them in the decision-making process. Paramount to the success of any organization is the investment of all who are employed. While leaders have the responsibility to share their vision and drive results, key strategies include building a foundation where there is support throughout the organization, from the top all the way to front line workers. Procedurally, organizations can engage workers by encouraging participation and motivating their efforts. This takes commitment from both the leader and the worker but allows both intrinsic and extrinsic rewards. This not only provides workers with compensation which may be tied to results but also impacts the worker personally. Organizational leaders who engage workers in the development process benefit from added value. Employees who are empowered and engaged in organizational development are metaphorically compared to the power of paper in the hands of an artist. While leaders are decisive and capable of getting the job done, workers who are engaged develop both personally and professionally while becoming more invested in helping the business grow. Leaders have a responsibility to empower followers and assist them to achieve their fullest potential.

TRANSPARENCY: CLEAR VISION REQUIRES CLEAR COMMUNICATION

"The art of communication is the language of leadership."
~James Humes

Organizational leaders affect change when the purpose is communicated to organizational members. This suggests organizational leaders are clear on the what, how, and why of organizational change for change to be effective. Leaders who are in the position to empower and elevate future leaders must first engage with those they are attempting to lead. In fact, it is suggested that leaders to keep an open-door policy. Having an open-door policy communicates to followers that their leader is approachable. It further signifies concern and care for those who are tasked with doing the work. When leaders are approachable they establish a climate of trust that allows for open communication. Effective communication is a necessary tool that fosters collaboration and allows organizational success. For this reason, effective communication in the workplace is essential. To ensure the efficiency of daily operations, organizational leaders should make certain to use clarity when communicating the goals of an organization. Communication should cross vertical as well as horizontal lines. Regardless of the industry, transparency is key to ensure everyone has an awareness of all vital information and updates accordingly. Therefore, both timely and frequent communication is required. While effective communication is one of the most important tasks for a leader, this is not always an easy.

Leaders of institutions such as education, hospitals, armed forces, and public sectors all face challenges when it comes to communicating effectively. The use of technology also plays an integral part in communication and collaboration within organizations. To maintain a pace congruent with growing organizations and global demands, business leaders understand the urgency of the use of technology.

Communication is especially important for leaders and followers when changing management. For a business to continue its success and effectively carry out the mission of the organization, leaders must ensure that a viable succession plan is in place. The bottom line for organizational success is the ability to maintain continuity despite organizational changes. Since leaders create organizational culture from their values, assumptions, and experiences, a succession plan is necessary and should be communicated when considering the succession of a founder. While organizational change can be good, communication reduces the anxiety that workers may have. For example, the new CEO of Ford Motors, Mark Fields, has been recognized for his decision to maintain the day-to-operations the same as his successor, Alan Mullaly. Mullaly is known for making a tremendous impact on a failing company that was close to filing for bankruptcy. Much of its demise, according to reports, was due to the organizational culture prior to Mullaly fulfilling the role of CEO in 2006 (Schein, 2010, p. 63).

To foster collaboration amongst various teams within an organization and ensure that each can function cohesively, leaders will need to incorporate the 4 C's: Communication, Collaboration, Creativity, and Commitment

- Communication – leaders must facilitate the ongoing exchange of thoughts and ideas between leaders and subordinates to discuss concepts for meeting the goals of the department
- Collaboration – the leaders for each department would work together to foster a collective approach to meeting each department's need while focusing on the overall mission of the organization

- Creativity – individual teams should seek opportunities to be innovative and bring forth new ideas and initiatives to reach their individual and departmental goals
- Commitment – all members of the team should be compelled to continue nurturing the newly developed alliances as the team forges ahead toward organizational success

(Author's Research)

The 4 C's are interchangeable pieces of a puzzle that are suitable for different departmental units and organizational members. As members of the organization work to fulfill personal and professional goals, this concept will help to create a solid structure, stable culture, and successful organization.

LEADERSHIP DEVELOPMENT

Since it is necessary to maintain highly effective leaders, organizations have begun to recognize the need to broaden the scope of investing in leaders. Beyond leadership development initiatives, organizations also seek to implement various processes, practices, and activities. With this in mind, organizations utilize leadership development systems that provide a framework for continuous performance improvement, succession management, and organizational change. For example, GlaxoSmithKline launched the Center of Excellence that provides a premier approach for entry-level management as well as for senior-level management to be further developed while encountering organizational transformation. Through these systems, leadership capacities are enhanced, and characteristics are revealed.

To ensure that the right people are in the right place with the right skills, many organizations invest in their leaders by implementing leadership development programs. This builds upon a leader's ability to be effective and efficient in their current role. Additionally, leadership development programs help build the leader's capacity to withstand organizational changes as well as prepare for continued advancement. Many organizations consider leadership development programs to be an effective strategy. Leadership development systems help to define core competencies necessary for leaders and the implications that these key competencies have on the effectiveness of the organization. Competency models promote a shared understanding of what effective leadership should look like while also creating the standard in which the leader should be measured. When leaders reflect on their values, those characteristics are demonstrated through their behaviors. In other words, a core competency for leaders is the ability to lead with their heart which, when connected to God, allows them to remain humble.

Since leadership development needs change over time, it is necessary to adopt an approach that will be most effective in achieving the intended results. When seeking leadership development options, organizations may consider providing either a performance coach or a life coach to work with their leaders. This involves a plan that includes participation and efforts on the part of the manager, implementation of an action plan, additional coaching, a formal feedback process, and an assessment phase. However, due to growth and expansion, organizations are becoming increasingly diverse. This presents new challenges for many leaders, particularly concerning global leadership. For this reason, traditional methods of leadership development are extinct. Today's leaders must seek to empower workers by developing competencies and a higher level of proficiency. This requires organizations to continually develop their leaders. As a result, leadership development will enhance the capacity of individuals and organizations.

An age-old debate exists regarding the innate capabilities of leaders. However, research suggests that leadership is nurtured through a developmental process. When organizations employ leadership development programs, it highlights the fact that talent comes first, and strategy comes second. From this perspective, each position is filled with the best person to fulfill the role and allow the team to thrive. Today's leaders recognize the need to cultivate a team approach. By doing this, it establishes a climate of trust and allows open communication. These values are necessary for team development and require leadership that will nurture these ideals. It further demands a focused approach to daily behavior towards improvement. In sports, for example, the coach would continually push players to play their hardest and continue winning games even if the team is on a winning streak. The future success of the team remains as important as the current winning status. Similarly, in business, sustainability is as important as momentarily beating the competition.

Coaching as a Strategy

Due to a paradigm shift, leadership development can be accomplished through coaching. Coaching is observed as a process by which leaders can guide followers in completing specific goals while empowering and developing as opposed to being self-absorbed and taking full credit for the success of the organization (Ciulla, 2014, p 49). While there is a historical context that ranges from a horse-drawn vehicle to that of an athletic nature, coaching metaphorically describes the ability to carry someone from point to another. Though coaching is vastly used in modern society for both individuals and organizations, Biblical examples illustrate the relationship between the coach and the client that has occurred throughout history. While a performance coach would focus on deficits and work towards improving the leader's performance in those identified areas, a life coach would involve a more holistic approach. In other words, using a life coach for leadership development is advantageous for organizations.

Leaders who serve as coaches authentically help to shape the lives of other individuals. Since coaching is a style of leadership that lends itself to viewing the performance of the team as a whole, this can be a pivotal aspect of measuring performance outcomes within organizations. Coaching leadership allows leaders to develop their followers and empower them to work as a team. While there are distinctions across varying industries, coaching promotes a team concept that drives results in both the business and sports world. In the business world, coaches strive to improve the overall effectiveness of the leader and his followers. This is also seen in the sports arena as players are developed into contributing members of their respective teams. While team-building exercises are not considered to be viable strategies for sustainability, coaching leadership does offer sustainable performance improvement. This has resulted in the emergence of coaching as a style of leadership. This is particularly significant as the leader's style is often adapted to fit the needs of an organization.

Leading Across Cultures

As companies spread globally, leaders must be prepared to lead across cultures. This requires the ability to handle conflicts concerning differences in histories, experiences, values, and cultures. In turn, leaders will be knowledgeable when working with collective groups with social identity differences such as race, gender, culture or religion. Effective methods to integrate groups of people and guide them towards accomplishing team goals must be carefully considered and executed.

While there is an ongoing debate about whether global leaders can transfer values when leading across various cultures, the success of the leader will be dependent upon the leader's character and capabilities. When leaders allow themselves to grow and develop, particularly in unfamiliar territory, this benefits the global leader as well as the business. Engaging a global mindset means having increased psychological, intellectual, and social capital. Having a global mindset enhances the capacity of the organization to expand across cultures while increasing potential profit. Leaders who maintain a global mindset while exhibiting key cross-cultural competencies are an asset for any organization and will allow them to be successful when leading across cultures.

Many individuals believe that they must maintain a work persona that is distinguished from their actual identity. In other words, individuals often feel they must keep their personal life separate from their professional life as well as keep their work-life separate from their identity. In actuality, work identities are not merely a reflection of an employee's role and responsibilities. While an employee's nationality, race, gender, language, religion, generation, and sexual orientation are nonprofessional identities, these attributes make up the individual's social identity and are key factors in the work environment. For example, effective leadership requires leaders to have a sense of self-awareness. This allows leaders to understand their ability to empower and influence others which ultimately helps to build the capacity of individuals while enhancing the overall performance of the organization. As organizations grow, social identity is increasingly important. I Corinthians 1:28 reminds us "God chose what is low and despised in the world, even things that are not, to bring things that are." This is a reminder that God can use anyone, even those who may be different. Social identity is integral to group formation within organizations. Social identity is described as a social process of interwoven identities individually, interactional, and institutionally. This perspective highlights the relationships between similar individuals as well as those who may be different. It further illustrates the interaction between employees who are empowered by leaders with whom they identify through categorization. This self-identification plays a pivotal role in how individuals see themselves and how they respond to others. With this in mind, leaders must be strategic in their approach to build and strengthen their teams.

The Crane Principle: How to Overcome Obstacles and Implement Organizational Change

Today's leaders face many challenges. Leaders are responsible for the growth and development of businesses. Leaders must also guide a team of productive workers while delivering quality service to customers and all stakeholders. Yet, as the world evolves, the need for growth and innovation becomes increasingly necessary. Due to technological advances as well as other external factors, many organizations are constantly and consistently in a state of changing their mission, purpose, or their normal way of doing business. In other words, organizations should consider changing their mission, expanding services, developing additional products, or increasing their client base. While change may be considered by some as a disturbance of the status quo (Kotter & Schlesinger, 2008) others view change as an opportunity to increase viability, revenue, and even resources. However, on one hand, employees perceive change as a threat to their livelihood and therefore challenge anything that is remotely different than what they are accustomed to and familiar with (Kotter & Schlesinger, 2008). On the other hand, organizational leaders must decide what, if anything, needs to change and then determine the necessary steps in order to ensure change readiness along with positive outcomes. This paper will thoroughly examine issues that organizational leaders face when attempting to initiate changes and offer suggestions to overcome those obstacles. The Crane Principle is an efficient process for organizational leaders when considering organizational changes to take their businesses to the next level.

Understanding the Need for Change

Today's leaders face many challenges when trying to sustain as well as gain an edge over the competition. Due to an ever growing economy and technological advances along with other external factors, organizations are constantly and consistently in a state of changing their mission, purpose, or their normal way of doing business. Organizational change can be best described as adjustments to the normal flow of operations and the management of those changes through planned and strategic measures by organizational leaders (Shin, Taylor, & Seo, 2012). Leaders may be prompted to make organizational changes for various reasons. For example, transformations could be as major as changing the mission of an organization or as minor as discontinuing a product (Burke, 2018). This could also occur in large or small organizations as well as across different industries. Many industries including the military, churches, for-profit organizations, and nonprofit organizations have been making organizational changes and embraced organizational development since the mid-1950s (Burke, 2018). To successfully manage and implement organizational changes, leaders have a lot to consider. One of the first things that leaders must consider are elements which may impact the organization's ability to initiate change. Leaders affect change when the purpose is clearly communicated to organizational members. This suggests that organizational leaders are clear on the what, how, and why of organizational change for change to be effective (Burke, 2018). Organizational leaders should be prepared to identify and address any issues that may arise and impact the organization's ability to initiate change.

In order to effectively implement change organizational leaders must be sure to recognize, diagnose, and address any gaps which may exist between intended organization change and the capacity of organizational members to perform once the changes are made (Miller & Proctor, 2016). Paying particular attention to the organizational change gap allows leaders to prepare for their organization's continuous change (Miller & Proctor, 2016). This is inclusive of generational gaps in the workplace which span over three to four generations (Shah, 2011). Leaders must be able to effectively communicate with organizational members from senior management level to front line workers to convey the mission of the organization as well as guide the organizational change process. Due to the age gap, leaders may have to be change agents for behavior. While it may be impossible to make people subscribe to a set of values they are not accustomed to, leaders can be effective in helping employees see the value in changing their behavior (Schein, 2010). Successful leaders can affect behavioral change, ultimately leading to changes in beliefs, attitudes, and values (Schein, 2010). Key factors will be examined to determine how organizational leaders can employ strategies to overcome obstacles and initiate changes.

Obstacles Impacting Organizational Change Initiatives

Organizational change can be successful but not often without its set of challenges. While processes are implemented to ensure efficiency, it does not account for unpredictable factors, such as human behavior and unintended outcomes. Though change leaders are visionaries and are able to see the benefits of changing the mission of an organization, the employees may observe changes as something that is complex and disrupts the organization (Denning, 2012). When resistance occurs, this may reveal systemic issues within the organization regarding organizational culture. Though changes in the culture may be necessary, it is a difficult task to change either group members' or individuals' behavior (Sims, 2000). The culture of an organization has a significant impact on establishing a climate which fosters and nurtures how individual ethics and behaviors are formed (Sims, 2000). While establishing the culture, leaders must also ensure appropriate planning of the change process to avoid negatively impacting organizational change. Although it may be the leader's intention to maximize resources and expand the organization (Castillo, Fernandez, & Jose, 2018), the leader's efforts could have an adverse effect. For example, instead of the intended results, the organizational change could cause low productivity, poor morale, and little to no job satisfaction of employees (Castillo, Fernandez, & Jose, 2018). However, the goal would be to become innovative, further grow the business, and thrive.

Facing giants: employees' attitudes and behaviors

Workers foresee change as an intrusive infringement upon their social relationships within the organization (Shin, Taylor, & Seo, 2012). Even in the midst of organizational change, the culture within the organization may shift. Though leaders may observe certain reactions to organizational change prior to the changes occurring, change leaders often do not anticipate dealing with behaviors after the change process is completed (Burke, 2018). It is common for organizational changes to evoke emotions which drives behaviors (Burke, 2018). For example, workers may view changes as an opportunity for professional growth in terms of a promotion and even higher pay. The anticipation and excitement of an increase in salary and a higher position is motivation to embrace organizational change and work fervently to ensure its success. The afore-mentioned example parallels with the notion that extrinsic rewards such as money and titles impact a person's actions (De Charms, 1983). Regardless of the reaction to change, organizational change continually occurs and gets even more complex depending on a company's size and structure. Change leaders must be cognizant of behaviors that are not altered after implementation of new goals and means and reward and control systems (Schein, 2010). The trick for organizational leaders is being able to move past the resistance to avoid devastating outcomes for organizations that find themselves facing difficult times (Denning, 2012).

When preparing for organizational change, leaders must consider the person-to-person interactions within their organizations. For larger enterprises, this adds an additional layer of concerns when considering the impact that organizational change can have on its members collectively as well as individually (Burke, 2018). To assist organizational members with their transition throughout the organizational change process, change leaders will need to focus on bridging the relationship between vision and action (Burke, 2018). This one step aligns thought and behavior so that organizational members are aware of the mission, purpose, and expected outcomes. When leaders are able to work through resistance and obtain commitment from workers, the organizational change process can begin.

Ready, get set, go.

Another critical factor for organizational leaders to consider is determining when would be an opportune time to make organizational changes. This means that leaders must assess organizational change readiness by examining the members' willingness to embrace change (Burke, 2018). In other words, leaders must gauge their employees' level of motivation and be prepared to unpack their current mindset (Burke, 2018). To do this, leaders may employ several strategies. These strategies may include providing data which reveals organizational performance versus performance needs based on market trends (Burke, 2018). Additionally, leaders will need to ensure that their team has the capacity to do what will be required of them once the changes occur. With this in mind, organizational members must also believe in their ability to successfully implement the desired changes (Weiner, 2009). While employees must be willing to implement changes (change commitment) and have the capacity to make these changes (change efficacy), it is also critically important for employees to see the value that organizational change offers (Weiner, 2009). Change commitment helps to shape the organizational culture needed to successfully persevere throughout the change process. Organizational change readiness can increase the likelihood of positive results when organizational changes are implemented. However, there are no guarantees that organizations that are willing to make organizational changes, will be able to do so successfully. This means that while an organization may be ready for change and is capable of implementing the required changes, organizational changes will not be successful if the plans are inadequate or poorly designed (Weiner, 2009). When leaders consider these factors, it increases the potential for organizational change to have positive results. The next step for leaders is determining which organizational change methods will be most effective.

The Crane Principle

As leaders seek to implement changes, considerations must extend beyond determining organizational readiness, but should also include concrete methods for implementing organizational changes. A deep dive is often necessary to examine all possible solutions that could be instrumental in beginning the organizational change process. This requires out of the box thinking. For example, this writer recalls a television show from the early 1990's by the name of Frasier. Each episode contained client concerns that needed to be resolved. The title of the show was developed from the main character on the show, Dr. Frasier Crane. The show was one of the longest aired sitcoms and portrayed the life of Dr. Crane throughout his personal and professional life. Dr. Crane was a psychologist who worked at a radio station and, in his role, offered advice to callers about various problems. Dr. Crane not only offered sage advice to his audience while managing relationships with his boss and colleagues, but he also had to contend with varying issues which ranged from caring for his aging father, being a positive influence on his younger brother, and trying to balance his own social life. In the ten plus years that the show aired many lessons were attained that leaders, regardless of their industry, could use when attempting to initiate change within their organizations.

In this role, Dr. Frasier Crane utilized various tactics to navigate his life. In doing so, he addresses the concerns of his work family, audience, and biological family. During each episode, Dr. Crane would always identify the issues and diagnose the problem then draw from his expertise and solve the problem. When using his skills to help others, Dr. Crane often used anecdotes to relate to others as well as iterate key points. His character is much like that of an organizational leader who guides and directs the mission of an organization while addressing the concerns of internal and external customers as well as stakeholders. The Crane principle demonstrates how organizational leaders impact the organizational change process when they can 1) identify, 2) diagnose, 3) strategize, and 4) solve problems.

- Identify – Leaders should be aware of issues within the organization and be able to highlight matters of concern that could negatively impact the organizational change process.
- Diagnose – Leaders must be able to determine the causes or reasons for resistance to change as well as overcome any obstacles.
- Strategize – Leaders should work to develop solutions for overcoming obstacles which would prevent changes occurring within the organization.
- Solve – Organizational leaders must determine the best solution for implementing organizational changes then execute the plan.

Figure 1.
THE CRANE PRINCIPLE

While organizational leaders use innovation and creativity to maintain sustainability as well as gain a competitive edge over others in the same industry, leaders find themselves having to be creative in their approach to implementing change. While there is no strategy that is guaranteed or foolproof, leaders must seek to determine effective methods that will be instrumental in allowing them to move forward as an organization. Many questions are raised when pondering which methods will benefit the organization. How can leaders address issues of employees' attitude and behavior towards organizational change? What strategies should leaders use to prepare organizations for change? Utilizing the Crane Principle is an effective strategy for organizational leaders when considering organizational changes to take their businesses to the next level.

Applying the Crane Principle

Organizational leaders can address concerns regarding employee attitudes and behaviors by working to build upon the organization's resources. For this to occur, leaders need to be aware that the changes may require additional resources and then look for ways to address this concern. By increasing company resources, this reduces the level of employees' stress caused by organizational change while increasing their level of commitment to change (Shin, Taylor, & Seo, 2012). There are two types of commitment that are mentioned with regard to organizational change. The first type of commitment is a normative commitment which means that employees will be committed to organizational change due to their sense of obligation as employees (Shin, Taylor, & Seo, 2012). Conversely, the other type of commitment, referred to as affective commitment, is demonstrated through employees' belief in the changes and how the organization will benefit from the changes (Shin, Taylor, & Seo, 2012).

When organizational leaders recognize resistance to change and can diagnose the reasons for the opposition, they will have to employ strategic methods that will allow employees to be at ease and embrace organizational change. Leaders employ many different strategies when attempting to gain 'buy-in' from organization members. One strategy is the use of storytelling. Storytelling can be a key strategy to utilize when preparing organizations for change. Another strategy when attempting to influence workers toward organizational change is for leaders to use written communication. While visual methods such as charts, and emails are presumably helpful for organization members to see what change could look like, this may not be the most effective. This works in some cases but may not work in every situation. However, research supports that storytelling proves to be a more effective strategy when making a major change in the workplace (Weiner, 2009). By providing a narrative of what change will look like and why it needs to occur, organizational leaders decrease employees' stress level while increasing their commitment to change. Storytelling provides a creative means for leaders to encourage enthusiasm and cooperation versus having to force compliance or terminate both managerial and frontline workers (Weiner, 2009). With storytelling, change leaders appeal to the psyche of organizational members which impacts their view of the change process (Weiner, 2009). When this occurs, it catapults the organization's readiness to reinvent itself (Weiner, 2009). This then allows for the successful implementation of change which includes the attitude and behavior of employees even after the changes have occurred. Since employees play a vital role in the success or failure of organizational change, leaders must be strategic in developing a plan of action to address employees' resistance to change. These strategies will further allow leaders to move forward with initiating organizational change while changing behavior at the same time.

The change in individuals may be accredited to Organizational Citizenship Behavior (OCB) (Choi, 2007). With this change, an individual becomes motivated to perform as an individual as well as a contributing member of the team. This motivation allows the individual to be both innovative and creative to increase overall performance. The idea of OCB aligns with the notion of employees becoming psychologically empowered to change (Choi, 2007). While the motivation for this change may be relative to personal achievement, it counterintuitively works in the organization's favor. At the same time, storytelling is an effective strategy that strengthens the connection between leaders and followers. Storytelling further compels workers to become motivated towards organizational change. Regardless of the reason for the motivation, change leaders can benefit from the changed attitudes and commitment to go through the change process.

SUMMARY

Leadership involves the honest guidance and training led by a visionary capable of persuading others to buy into the organizational mission and values. The call to leadership not only requires the ability to persuade, or influence, individuals toward a specific goal but to do so while portraying the characteristics of the ultimate leader, Jesus Christ. Leadership, by definition, dictates that one or more persons are directed towards accomplishing an assigned task. In doing so, leaders and followers coexist and are inter-dependent upon one another to have a cohesive team. While several theories seek to explain various leadership styles and their impact on how organizations function, it is the leadership style of the leader that plays an integral role in being able to sustain as well as transform an organization. To achieve the mission of an organization, leaders must consider their most important resources, their workers. The team leadership model explains the team concept is fundamental to an organization's overall effectiveness. This model focuses on the functional leader approach which views the leader as possessing the responsibility of operating to achieve organizational success. This team approach encourages both engagement and collaboration.

There is a correlation between one's leadership style and the ability to engage workers. To strengthen the leader-follower relationship, organizational leaders must be sure to model the behavior that they expect, revealing their true character. In other words, effective leaders are those who are capable of inspiring others based on who they are and not just what they do. Essentially, these leadership characteristics are motivators that help drive employee behavior. Key strategies for leaders to be successful in their leadership roles include leading with both the heart and mind. Successful leaders will also maintain key characteristics that will strengthen the capacity of the organization. These qualities include humility, empathy, agility, responsibility, and transparency. When leaders operate by demonstrating their core values, followers can adopt the same espoused values. When this occurs, the leader-follower relationship is enhanced while impacting overall performance and, ultimately, meeting the goals of the organization.

To effectively meet the goals of an organization, the leader must be able to coach followers while managing the productivity of the organization. Therefore, self-awareness is critical for leaders when to be able to make sound decisions. While leadership positions are highly regarded and sought after, the call to leadership requires leaders to gain self-awareness of their personal qualities and skills. Knowledge of these key strategies assists leaders with personal development as well as global leadership. Today's leaders face many challenges when trying to sustain as well as gain a competitive edge over others in the industry. For this reason, leaders should continually seek to innovate. Due to an ever-growing economy and technological advances along with other external factors, organizational leaders are consistently having to change their mission, purpose, or their way of doing 'business as usual'. Organizational change can be best described as adjustments to the normal flow of operations and the management of those changes through planned and strategic measures by organizational leaders. Many leaders are prompted to make organizational changes for various reasons. These transformations could be as major as changing the mission of an organization or as minor as discontinuing a product and may occur in large or small organizations as well as across different industries.

Several examples exist in the Bible that demonstrates how man is to live Christ-like. Through scriptures, the true characteristics of Christ are revealed while lessons for humankind are demonstrated as well. Lessons revealed through scripture catalyzes further understanding of how Christians are led to go into the world and bring others to Christ. An interpretation of God using Paul in Philippians 2 demonstrates the power of Paul's message to the people of Philippi. In his letters, the Apostle Paul appeals to the core of the Christians: their values and beliefs. The people of Philippi were encouraged by Paul to live Christ-filled lives which was modeled for all to follow. Paul wanted the Philippians to realize that, if they continually seek to remain humble and put others before themselves, their Christ-like characteristics will honor God and allow Him to be glorified on earth as well as in heaven. Through lessons learned from Christ, Paul allowed his life to exemplify Christ, demonstrating a basis for allowing leaders to lead for the benefit of others. This is also relevant for today's leaders. Once leaders learn that leadership is serving, only then can leaders truly serve God and fulfill their calling. Paul's love for Christ, as depicted in the scripture, demonstrated his willingness to remain humble and be a servant-leader. Today's leaders can fellowship and be restored in a place of worship. The church, ultimately, is symbolic of a launching pad for Christian leaders to continuously be inspired by scripture and led by the Holy Spirit to lead others. Leaders are reminded in I Corinthians 12:13.1 that "For in one Spirit we were all baptized into one body-Jews or Greeks, slaves or free-and all were made to drink of one Spirit". With this in mind, Christian leaders can be inspired to lead across cultures and capable of successful global leadership.

Leaders are prompted to make organizational changes for various reasons. For organizations to sustain as well as grow, leaders will have to consider changing the mission, purpose, or the usual way of doing business. While organizational change is necessary it can also be challenging. Even though processes may be put into place to ensure efficiency, it cannot predict factors such as human behavior and negative outcomes. Successful management and implementation of the organizational change process requires leaders to make careful considerations. For leaders, one of the many things to consider are elements which may impact the organization's ability to initiate change. The leader affects change when they clearly communicate the purpose and plan for all organizational members. Additionally, when leaders ensure organizational change readiness, the likelihood for positive results are increased. Though organizational change readiness does not necessarily predict the outcome in all cases, the chances are greater for those organizations that are prepared. Successful organizational leaders decide what needs to change and then take the necessary steps to initiate those changes. In order to overcome obstacles which may prevent changes from occurring, organizational leaders should consider utilizing the Crane Principle. In doing so, leaders will be able to identify the issues, diagnose problems, implement a strategy, and then solve the issues, ultimately, effecting change. Change leaders are effective when they can recognize resistance, diagnose reasons for the opposition, and then employ strategic methods that will allow employees to be at ease and embrace organizational change. A key strategy for organizational leaders is storytelling. Storytelling can be a critical component when preparing organizations for change. While communicating by using visuals such as charts, emails, and other forms of written communication may be helpful to show organization members what change could look like, it does not allow for two-way communication which would allow employees to ask questions of the leaders directly and receive a response. Employees play a vital role in the success or failure of the organization. This holds true throughout the change process as well. For this reason, leaders must be strategic in developing a plan of action to address employees' resistance to change. These strategies allow leaders to move forward with initiating organizational change while simultaneously changing behavior. The Crane Principle allows organizational leaders to initiate changes and have the desired outcome.

Though the military and churches have been making organizational changes since the mid-1950s, other industries have embraced organizational development as well, including for-profit and non-profit organizations. To successfully manage and implement organizational changes, leaders have a lot to consider. One of the first things that leaders must consider is elements that may impact the organization's ability to initiate change. Leaders effect change when the purpose is communicated to organizational members. This suggests that organizational leaders are clear on the what, how, and why of organizational change for change to be effective. Determining what the change goals are is just as important as deciding the methods for creating change. Most importantly, organizational leaders should be prepared to identify and address any issues that may arise and impact the organization's ability to initiate change.

To effectively implement change, organizational leaders must be sure to recognize, diagnose, and address any gaps which may exist between intended organizational change and the capacity of organizational members to perform once the changes are made. Paying particular attention to the organizational change gap allows leaders to prepare for their organization's continuous change. This is inclusive of generational gaps in the workplace which span over three to four generations. To engage multigenerational followers, leaders must be able to effectively communicate with all levels, demographics, and ages. This will require leaders to have a certain skillset which engages all members within the organization while fostering an environment of collaboration. While it may be impossible to require people to subscribe to a set of values in which they are unaccustomed, leaders can be effective in helping employees see the value in being open to change. These include changes in beliefs, attitudes, values, and even behavior. Further understanding of key factors have determined when organizational leaders lead with their heart, they can employ strategies to overcome obstacles and initiate changes.

Organizational change can be best described as adjustments to the normal flow of operations and the management of those changes through planned and strategic measures by organizational leaders. Many leaders are prompted to make organizational changes for various reasons. Transformations could be as major as changing the mission of an organization or as minor as discontinuing a product. This may occur in large or small organizations and across different industries. Regardless of the size of the organization, leaders must develop skills and adopt a leadership style that will allow him or her to meet organizational goals. Several leadership styles describe characteristics that relate to the behaviors of leaders. Transformational Leadership is observed as a style of leadership whereby the leader engages with others in order to create a connection which establishes a level of trust, allowing both leader and follower to be motivated. Authentic leadership is based on faith in leadership and is first seeded by the leader's character in alignment with Proverbs 24:5-6 which reveals "A wise man has great power, and a man of knowledge increases strength." Transactional Leadership is described as a style that fosters an exchange between leaders and their followers. The leader-follower relationship has a direct impact on both the climate and the productivity of an organization. The significance of this pivotal aspect can be measured by performance outcomes seen within organizations.

Successful leaders understand that organizations need a roadmap to help guide the mission of their organizations. To do this, leaders develop a strategy for the organization, using the structure as a vehicle. From this perspective, organizational design and strategy are interconnected. Key factors such as wisdom, experience, and individual employee perspectives are drivers that help to ensure organizations reach optimal success. Virtuous leaders are led by habits of both the heart and the mind. One of the cardinal virtues which drive behavior is wisdom. Wisdom is considered to be the master virtue that allows leaders to use good judgment, be decisive, and discern correctly. This comes with both maturities as well as a change in mindset. While using past experiences as a basis for determining future outcomes, organizational leaders can be creative and develop strategies that allow for sustainability while maintaining a competitive edge. To do this effectively, leaders must be cognizant of both internal and external factors which may impact the strategy-making process. With this in mind, leaders will determine whether to adopt an inside-out approach or outside-in way in which to develop a strategy. This means the leader will be required to decide whether to build a strategy conducive for the internal environment that must be able to adapt to the outside world, or, conversely, design a strategy that appeases all stakeholders in which organizational members must be able to embrace. Regardless of the approach, leaders must communicate organizational strategies and emphasize their priority. While an emphasis is placed on communicating and prioritizing organizational strategy, it is pivotal to recognize the significance of how strategy-making should be managed. To ensure strategy-making is both planned and purposeful, leaders must focus on behaviors on the future of the organization. Following scriptural instruction, wise leaders understand that "The plans of the diligent lead surely to abundance…" (Proverbs 21:5). This awareness begins with the leader understanding who they are as a leader or the type of leader they need to become.

As mentioned previously, the relationship between leaders and followers is significant in achieving any goal. Also illustrated is an understanding that self-awareness is an important factor in how one chooses to lead. Self-awareness should be a driving force that allows leaders to manage their lives as well as allow them to lead others. A keen sense of self allows leaders to identify areas of opportunity for growth. Therefore, self-awareness is critically important for leaders to be able to make a difference in their work, organization, and lives of their followers, thus, enhancing the necessary relationship needed for organizational success. The leadership style the leader possesses can have an impact on the organization and, ultimately, make a difference in the success of the organization. Besides having a sense of self-awareness, leaders who are cognizant of their role as a manager, are able to make an impression as a manager that is both positive and inspiring to followers. In essence, this provides an example for followers to emulate. Modeling the behavior expected of followers is considered to be more effective than just telling followers what's expected. Leaders who use impression management, articulate their values, and model intended behavior are able to inspire others to follow. While there is a clear distinction between leadership and management, the two words are often misunderstood and used interchangeably. From a sociological perspective, leaders are viewed by what they represent. In other words, leaders are observed, symbolically, as a social force that brings about change or social order.

As organizations grow and become increasingly diverse, leaders must be cognizant of the following: 1) know who they are, 2) understand organizational culture, 3) be aware of how their role integrates organizational culture, 4) identify ways to create shared culture within the organization, and 5) realize the significance of shared basic assumptions within their organization. As organizations evolve, the organizational culture must be adapted to ensure that the various subcultures within the organization can continue working collaboratively towards the mission. Due to the norms and customs across various cultures, a social order, or acceptable behavior, must be established to co-exist across cultures within the same industry. Leaders are the change agents responsible for the honest guidance and training of followers. As the visionary of the organization, leaders must be capable of persuading others to buy-in to the mission of an organization, particularly when merging two cultures. There are five practices of exemplary leadership which assist leaders in creating shared culture between two organizations. Utilizing these five practices, the leader will effectively set the tone by embedding the mission and the culture of the organization, helping to achieve long-term success.

Some scholars view charisma as an essential element of successful leadership. When one considers that organizations are reflections of the leaders, the outlook for businesses would appear to reflect a positive image. From this perspective, the scope of organizational success is narrowed by focusing solely on personality. This impression is tantamount to Christian leaders who are led by the Spirit and guided by Scripture. The impression left by Jesus reveals the true nature of the ultimate leader: servanthood. Christian theology seeks to reveal the divine nature of God and who He is in mankind. Biblical, historical, and theological aspects found in both the Old Testament and the New Testament explain God's true image. Jesus' leadership is also shown through the interaction between Him and his disciples. Scripture reveals the fundamental principle of God's leadership: love. In the gospel of John, great emphasis is placed on the word "love" and the promise of God (John 14:23) which states, "Those who love me will keep my word, and my Father will love them, and we will come to them and make our home with them." Believers are encouraged to show their love for Christ by remaining obedient to His word.

The heart is viewed as the vital center, or driving impulse, of the body. In comparison, the heart is to the body what the leader is to the organization. From this perspective, the leader is critical to the functioning of the organization and integral in steering the mission to achieve intended goals. Essentially, the leader is the heartbeat of the organization. When leaders recognize the impact that their leadership style has on the ability to influence workers plus learn to lead with humility, empathy, agility, responsibility, and transparency, leaders will then have a framework for building stronger teams, operating efficiently, and driving the mission of an organization.

APPENDIX

The following manifesto serves as an example of how organizations can make a declaration about their intentions for organizational operations. It further explicates a plan to ensure that the leadership style is guided by the H.E.A.R.T. of the leader to strengthen the capacity of their organization. While manifestos can be utilized across any industry, this example delineates a manifesto for a non-profit organization:

Leadership Manifesto

While the motivation to work varies according to the individual, the will to work is fused by divine inspiration. Hebrews 6:10 instructs us to serve Christ by *serving His people*. Working for a non-profit organization epitomizes true servanthood. Its ultimate product is neither a pair of shoes nor an effective regulation. Its product is a changed human being. Possessing the background and credentials may qualify a candidate to assume the leadership title, the role requires one to have the capacity to lead by example, inspire others toward change, and empower the next generation.

One of the key factors of effective leadership is the ability to demonstrate the behavior that is expected of followers. It is not enough for leaders to simply expect followers to listen to what I say but instead *watch what I do*. This philosophy of leading by example is a well-researched best practice to be implemented in any industry and serves group homes well when attempting to lead the next generation. Leading by example is one of the characteristics of *servant leaders*. As the Bible reminds us, we should not make efforts to be domineering over those in our charge, but rather be an example to the flock. Imagine being in a leadership position at a group home and one of the residents asks how is it that you can smile and keep the same attitude every when coming in to work. It is further remarkable that the resident appears to be in awe at how everyone is treated with dignity and respect, despite the behaviors displayed and issues encountered. These are the guiding principles of the group home that each staff must follow. The principles are also a testament to *show empathy to others*. Part of expressing empathy towards others is knowing who you are. Self-awareness is a critical element for leaders to be able to make a difference in their work, organization, and followers' lives. Self-awareness must also be the driving force that allows leaders to manage their lives and guide their organizations. As leaders, it is more effective to *show others the way*.

Leadership is best described as a leader's ability to persuade, or influence, individuals toward a specific goal. Leaders demonstrate effectiveness when they can inspire others and gain their buy-in, particularly when dealing with change. The role of leaders, as the world and organizations continue to evolve, is to become an agent for change. In other words, in an ever-evolving world, the leader is not only responsible for leading others but is also critical to the change process. As change agents, leaders will assume various roles, essentially wearing many hats while creating the structural stability, depth, breadth, and patterning or integration of the organization and its members. As a *change agent* for Serenity Group Home, the leader will demonstrate effectiveness by utilizing the following *five core capabilities*: 1) adaptive leadership; 2) executing single changes effectively; 3) managing the demand for change; 4) hiring resilient people, and; 5) creating the context for successful change. While the leader steers the efforts for each core capacity, the leader will engage every group home staff member to successfully build the context for change. Allowing workers to be engaged in the change process by giving their input creates a sense of value for each worker. Leadership will continually foster a sense of community, thereby influencing the shared values of group home staff members to *achieve organizational goals*.

Franklin D. Roosevelt's famous words, *"we cannot always build the future for our youth, but we can build our youth for the future"* is the resonating theme that inspires the mission of Serenity Group Home. We further believe in the need for leaders to *bring out the best* in their followers. For leaders to elevate followers, they must first ensure change readiness. While there is no guarantee of any particular strategy when preparing for organizational change readiness, it is up to the leader to determine when staff members are ready to implement change. For this reason, the Serenity Group Home leadership will increase the likelihood of positive results by implementing change principles. Utilizing change principles will allow leaders to be successful. Organizations are successful when they are led by highly effective leaders who seek to *build leaders*, not just followers. Building leaders require those in leadership to recognize they are not a one-man team and are only capable of achieving organizational goals through the work they inspire others to do. Leaders should further *swallow humility pills* and learn to see themselves as lowly co-laborers working alongside God versus having an ego that desires to take sole credit for every goal accomplished. For leaders to remain humble, it may require a change of heart. Former business owner, John Mackey, notes the longest journey people must take is the eighteen inches between their heads and their hearts (Mackey, 2014, p. 10). This change of heart transforms the leaders to care more about the success of the organization than about their comfort by empowering those that they lead. Serenity Group Home leaders will make sure to empower staff as well as youth that *as long as they have passion, faith, and are willing to work hard, they can do anything and have anything they want in this world.*

It is believed that leaders who live out their values, as well as model intended behavior, can inspire others to follow. It is further believed that leading by example and engaging workers in the change process helps to empower workers to become leaders. As Christian leaders, we should be inspired by Scripture, propelled by purpose, and willing to put our God-given talents to work. Leaders should strive to lead with compassion, inspire workers to become change agents and make every effort to achieve their fullest potential.

REFERENCES

Ackermann, F. and Eden, C. (2011). *Making strategy: Mapping out strategic success.* Thousand Oaks, CA: SAGE Publications.

Ayers, M (2006). Towards a Theology of Leadership. *Journal of Biblical Perspectives in Leadership.* Volume 1, Number 1, pp. 3-27.

Baker, M.N. (2014). Peer to Peer Leadership. San Francisco, CA: Berrett-Koehler.

Bartlett R. (2013). A practitioner's guide to business analytics: Using data analysis to improve your organization's decision making and strategy. USA: McGraw Hill.

Bekker, C.J. (2008). Leading with the head bowed down: Lessons in leadership humility from the rule of St. Benedict of Nursia. *Inner Resources for Leaders,* p. 1-10.

Belzung, C. (2014). empathy. Journal for Perspectives of Economic Political and Social Integration, 19(1), 177-191.

Briner, B. & Pritchard, R. (1997). The leadership lessons of Jesus. Nashville, TN: BH Publishing Group.

Burke, W.W. (2018). *Organization change.* Thousand Oaks, CA: Sage Publications, Inc.

Burton, R. M., Obel, B., & Hakonsson, D.D. (2015). *Organizational design: A step-by-step approach.* UK: Cambridge University Press.

Caliguiri, P. (2012). *Cultural agility: Building a pipeline of successful global professionals.* San Francisco, CA: Jossey-Bass.

Castillo, C. Fernandez, V., & Jose, M. (2018). The six emotional stages of organizational change. *Journal of Organizational Change Management 31*(3).

Cameron, K.S. & Quinn, R.E. (2011). *Diagnosing and changing organizational culture.* San Francisco, CA: Jossey-Bass. environment characteristics and intervening psychological processes. Journal of Organizational Behavior 28(4), pp. 467-484.

Collins, J. (2001). Good to great: *Why some companies make the leap... and others don't.* US: Harper Collins.

Cooke, J.A. (2010). From bean to cup: How Starbucks transformed its supply chain. *Supply Chain Quarterly.* Retrieved January 24, 2019.

Cunningham, L. (2015, 01 25). the secret sauce of corporate leadership. *the wall street journal.* Retrieved from http://www.wsj.com/articles/lawrence-a-.

Ciulla, J. B. (2014). *Ethics, the heart of leadership.* Santa Barbara, CA: Praeger.

Davenport, T.H, Harris, J.G., Morison, R. (2010). Analytics at work. USA: Harvard Business School Publishing Corporation.

De Charms, R. (1983). *Personal causation: The internal affective determinants of behavior.* Hillsdale, NJ: Lawrence Erlbaum Associates, Inc.

Denning, S. (2012). The Springboard: How storytelling ignites into action in knowledge-era organizations. (n.p.): Taylor & Francis.

Drucker, P.F. (2004). *The effective executive: The definitive guide to getting the right things done.* New York, NY: Harper Collins.

Dungy, T. & Whitaker, N. (2010). *The mentor leader.* Winter Park, FL: Tyndale House.

Duvall, J. S. & Hays, J.D. (2012). *Grasping God's word: A hands-on approach to reading, interpreting, and applying the Bible* (2nd Edition). Grand Rapids, MI: Zondervan Press

Faulhaber, J. (2008). *A biblical approach to developing the inner qualities of a leader.* USA: Xlibris Corporation.

Foot, P. (1997). Virtues and vices. *Virtue ethics,* 163-177.

Forgas, J.P. (1998). On being happy and mistaken. Mood effects on the fundamental attribution error. *Journal of Personality and Social Psychology, 75*(2), 318-331.

Gregersen, H.B. & Morrison, H.J. (1998). Developing Leaders for the Global Frontier. *Dialnet* (40)1.

Harvey, M. (2014). 3M. *The Safety & Health Practitioner, 32*(12), 51.

Heart. (n.d.). In *Merriam-Webster's collegiate dictionary.* Retrieved from https://www.merriam-webster.com/dictionary/heart.

Howes, L. (2018). Kobe Bryant: Mamba Mentality, NBA championships, and Oscars with Lewis Howes. {Video File}. Retrieved from https://www.youtube.com/watch?v=WY0wONSarXA.

Hughes, R. L., Beatty, K.C., and Dinwoodie, D.L. (2014). *Becoming a strategic leader.* (2nd Edition). San Francisco, CA: Jossey-Bass.

Hultman, K., & Gellermann, W. (2002). *Balancing individual and organizational values: Walking the tightrope to success.* San Francisco, CA: Jossey-Bass.

Kawasaki, G. (2004). *The art of the start.* USA: Penguin Group.

Keidel, R.W. (1994). Rethinking organizational design. *Academy of Management Executive 8*(4) pp. 12-28.

Kotter, J.P. and Schlesinger, L. A. (2008). Choosing strategies for change. Harvard Business Review. (130-139).

Kouzes, J. & Posner, B. (2012). The leadership challenge: How to make extraordinary things happen in organizations. San Francisco, CA: Jossey Bass.

Krull, D.S., Loy, M.H., Lin, J., Wang, C., Chen, S. & Zhao, X. (1999). The fundamental attribution error: Correspondence bias in individualist and collectivist cultures. Personality and Social Psychology Bulletin, 25 (1), 1208-1219.

Kuyper, A. (2011). Wisdom & wonder: common grace in science & art. Grand Rapids, MI: Christian's Library Press.

Leifer, R. (2000). *Radical innovation: How mature companies can outsmart upstarts.* Boston: Harvard Business School Press.

Lingenfelter, S.G. (2008). *Leading cross-culturally: Covenant relationships for effective Christian leadership.* Grand Rapids, MI: Baker Publishing Group.

McCauley, C.D., Kanaga, K., Lafferty, K. (2010). The center for creative leadership handbook of leadership development. San Francisco, CA: Jossey-Bass.

Mackenzie, I., & Welch, P. (2005). Leading from the heart. *Development and Learning in Organizations: An International Journal, 19*(1), 13-14.

Mackey, J. & Sisodia, R. (2013). *Conscious capitalism: Liberating the heroic spirit of business.* Boston, MA: Harvard Business School Publishing Corporation.

Manby, J. (2012). *Love works.* Grand Rapids, MI: Zondervan.

Manz, C.C. (1998). *The leadership wisdom of Jesus.* San Francisco, CA: Berrett-Koehler.

Maxwell, J. (2002). *Leadership 101: What every leader needs to know.* Nashville, TN: Thomas Nelson, Inc.

Miller, D. & Proctor, A. (2016). *Enterprise change management: how to prepare yourorganization for continuous change.* London, United Kingdom: Hogan Page.

Mintzberg, H. (1981). Organization design: fashion or fit. *Harvard Business Review.* pp. 103-116.

Murray, A. (2010). *The Wallstreet journal essential guide to management.* New York, NY: Harper-Collins.

n.d. (2012). EPA endorses 3M LeadCheck. *Home Channel News, 38*(5), 47.

Northouse, P.G. (2016). *Leadership: Theory and Practice* (7th ed.). Los Angeles, California: SAGE Publications, Inc.

Oster, G. (2011). *The light prize: Perspectives on Christian innovation.* Virginia Beach, VA: Positive Signs Media.

O'Toole, J. & Lawler, III, E.E. (2006). *The new American workplace.* New York, NY: Palgrave Macmillan.

Pavlovich, K., & Krahnke, K. (2014). Organizing through empathy. New York, NY: Routledge, Taylor & Francis Group.

Pfeiffer.Kouzes, J. & Posner, B. (2012). The leadership challenge: How to make extraordinary things happen in organizations. San Francisco, CA: Jossey-Bass.

Popper, M. (2005). Leaders who transform society. Westport, CT: Praeger.

Reid, B. (2012). Desirable leadership traits from the Old Testament. *Huffington Post*.

Ries, E. (2011). *The lean startup*. New York, NY: Crown Publishing Group.

Rindova, V.P. & Petkova, A.P. (2007). When is a new thing a good thing? Technological change, product form design, and perceptions of value for product innovations. *Organization Science, 18*(2), 217-232.

Rothwell, W.J. (2016). *Effective succession planning: Ensuring leadership continuity and building talent from within*. New York, NY: Amacom.

Schein, E.H. (2010). *Organizational culture and leadership*. San Francisco, CA: Jossey-Bass.

Schultz, H. & Yang, D.J. (1997). *Pour your heart into it: How Starbucks built a company one cup at a time*. New York, New York: Hyperion.

Shah, R. (2011). Working With Five Generations In The Workplace. *Forbes Magazine*.

Retrieved April 14, 2019, from http://www.forbes.com/sites/rawnshah/2011/04/20/working- with-five-generations-in-the-workplace.

Shin, J., Taylor, M.S., & Seo, M.G. (2012). Resources for change: The relationships of organizational inducements and psychological resilience to employees' attitudes and behaviors toward organizational change. *Academy of Management Journal 55*(2), p. 727-748.

Sims, R.R. (2000). Changing an organization's culture under new leadership. *Journal of Business Ethics 25,* 65-78.

Stark, D. (2005). *Christ-based leadership.* Grand Rapids, MI: Bethany House.

Stehlik, D. (2014). Ultimately contingent: Leveraging the power-web of culture, leadership, & organization design for effective innovation. *Journal of Strategic Leadership 5*(1), 10-22.

Vesper, K. (1993). *New venture mechanics.* Englewood Cliffs, NJ: Prentice-Hall, Inc.

Weiner, B.J. (2009). A theory of organizational readiness for change. *Implementation Science 4*(1), pp. 67-75.

Winston, B., and Patterson, K. (2006). An integrative definition of leadership. International *Journal of Leadership Studies*, 1(2), 6-66.

Wooden, J. {TED} (2009). The difference between winning and succeeding. {Video File}. Retrieved from https://www.youtube.com/watch?v=0MM-psvqiG8.

Wooden, J. & Carty, J. (2005). *Coach Wooden's pyramid of success.* Grand Rapids, MI: Baker Publishing Company.

ACKNOWLEDGEMENTS

A huge thank you to the many leaders who provided insight as well as inspiration for this writing. I will be forever grateful for the pastoral, educational, and familial encouragement and support that allowed me to take this amazing journey. I am deeply humbled and honored to be able to share various stories, experiences, and theories that have allowed me to develop as a leader.

A heartfelt thank you is extended to my Regent University family, especially Dr. Gary Oster and Dr. Diane Wiater for your tremendous support and guidance. To Dr. Kathleen Patterson (my Abuelo's buddy), thank you for your commitment and dedication to the development of leaders.

To my family and friends, there are no words that can express the gratitude I have for your unwavering love and support. You have faithfully remained in my corner despite my having to miss celebrations and gatherings. To my mother, Joann, thank you for always being my rock and for instilling in me the values that make me want to be a better person and leader. And finally, my son, Tyler. I love you beyond words. Thank you for always keeping me grounded. I am proud of the young man that you've become and look forward to seeing all that life has in store for you. May your life be richly blessed my son.

ABOUT THE AUTHOR

Dr. Carla D. Brown holds a doctoral degree in Strategic Leadership and currently serves as a Training and Development Director at the University of South Carolina as well as an Adjunct Professor for Regent University. Throughout her 25-year career, she has had an opportunity to work at every level of management across multiple industries. Dr. Brown utilizes her experiences to provide consultancy and training to impact workforce development. She lives in Columbia, SC and has a son, Tyler.

Printed in the United States
By Bookmasters